Make Me Clean

Make Me Clean

David E. Rosage

Lamp Press

Marshall Morgan and Scott
Lamp Press
34–42 Cleveland Street, London, W1P 5FB. UK.

ISBN 0 551 01912 3

Printed in Great Britain by Cox & Wyman Ltd, Reading

*Dedicated to all whose professional
or personal touch has brought healing
to others.*

Contents

Introduction

Written or spoken words are not only the usual way we communicate, they are also the most effective and most powerful vehicle for conveying our thoughts and feelings as well as other information. Words have a triple function. In the first place, they pass on information whether formally such as in a teaching situation or through ordinary conversation.

Second, they give us some insights into the personality of the speaker. They tell us something of the person's character, philosophy of life, interests, and prejudices.

Third, words have the potential of establishing a good or bad relationship between the speaker and the audience. If a speaker expresses gratitude for something we have done, we are pleased and appreciate the thoughtfulness of the person. In turn, this enriches our relationship with that person.

The words of Scripture fulfill the same triple function but in a much more profound way. The words of Scripture impart information of paramount importance for our spiritual welfare and eternal destiny. From the words of Scripture we learn the way of salvation.

Second, the words of Scripture reveal a great deal about our transcendent God: the Creator, the energizer, and the sustainer of the entire universe. Jesus is the Word of the Father. In proclaiming the Good News, Jesus reveals truths about the Godhead which we would not otherwise know. Divine revelation is not so much information about sacred truths as it is the unveiling of the nature of the God of love.

Third, from the words of Scripture we learn that God is a

loving, caring, providing God who loves us with an infinite love. He is a God who heals our hearts, relieves our pain, and comforts us in affliction. In three brief words, the apostle John reveals the nature of God. "God is love" (1 Jn 4:16). Jesus, in an equally brief statement, tells us of his own limitless love for us. "As the Father loves me, so I also love you. Remain in my love" (Jn 15:9).

Identity

In our utilitarian society, we have a great tendency to evaluate or judge people's worth by their accomplishments rather than by their qualities and gifts as a person. Too often we observe only the externals rather than the interior beauty of a personality.

Jesus was well aware of this attitude even in his own time. For this reason when the disciples of John the Baptist approached Jesus with the question: "Are you the one who is to come, or should we look for another?" Jesus simply identified himself with his accomplishments. Jesus called their attention to his divine healing power. "Go and tell John what you hear and see: the blind regain their sight, the lame walk, lepers are cleansed, the deaf hear, the dead are raised, and the poor have the good news proclaimed to them" (Mt 11:3-5).

Jesus began his public ministry by healing many types of infirmity or affliction which he encountered in everyday life. He wanted to be known as a healer, not so much to manifest his divine power as to reveal his boundless love.

After the resurrection when Jesus met the two disciples on the road to Emmaus, he identified himself as the one who had fulfilled all the prophecies about the Messiah. "Then beginning with Moses and all the prophets, he interpreted to them what referred to him in all the scriptures" (Lk 24:27). By fulfilling these prophecies Jesus proved beyond any shadow of a doubt that he was the long-expected Messiah, the promised Savior of the world.

At the outset of Jesus' public ministry, however, when the

disciples of John the Baptist came to him, the prophecies had not yet been fulfilled in him. For this reason Jesus did not appeal to them as proof of his divine mission. At that time his healing ministry showed his divine power and compassionate love. This is why Jesus identified himself only as a divine healer at the beginning of his public ministry.

Multiple Cures

We will never be able to calculate the number of healings which Jesus wrought. Throughout the pages of Scripture, from Genesis to Revelation, we find occasions of divine healings. The Gospels are full of accounts of healings which Jesus performed for a certain person or for a whole group. In addition we are told that Jesus healed all who were brought to him. In Matthew alone we read: "He . . . cured all the sick" (Mt 8:16) and "Jesus went around to all the towns and villages . . . curing every disease and illness" (Mt 9:35). And again, "People brought to him all those who were sick . . . and as many as touched it [the tassel on his cloak] were healed" (Mt 14:35ff). And yet again: "Great crowds came to him, having with them the lame, the blind, the deformed, the mute, and many others. They placed them at his feet, and he cured them" (Mt 15:30). We find similar accounts in the other Gospels as well.

As Jesus trudged down the dusty paths and roads of Palestine to reach out in healing love to all he met, no exact accounts of all his healings were recorded. Even if there had been any attempt to do so, the many inner healings which undoubtedly took place could never have been made visible or known. With the exception of a few accounts, we have no idea how many conversions took place. Nor could we count the peace, the joy, the hope, and encouragement which filled the hearts of the many who came to him begging for a healing.

We need to recall that Jesus always healed the whole person and not merely physical ailments. When the four men brought the paralytic to Jesus, they asked only for a physical healing, but

Jesus healed the whole person when he said: "Child, your sins are forgiven" (Mk 2:5). When Jesus arrived on the scene and drove out the demons of hatred, prejudice, anger, and bitterness—a whole host of other evil phenomena were likewise dispelled from the lives of those who had been crippled spiritually and physically. We have no record of the number of these inner healings worked by Jesus as the compassionate healer of God's people. But they aptly demonstrate that Jesus always sought to heal the whole person and not just one isolated physical or emotional problem.

His Presence Heals

Jesus' very presence brought healing to many. Throughout his earthly sojourn, the presence of Jesus brought deep inner healing to the wounded. This healing was accompanied by great joy, peace, and calm.

We recall his first miracle at the wedding feast in Cana. In responding to the intercession of his mother and the cooperation of the attendants, Jesus—by his presence and power—avoided much embarrassment to the wedding party and also contributed to the merriment of the guests.

Likewise, his presence brought great healing to the frightened disciples as he walked across the water on the Sea of Galilee in the midst of a terrible storm (Jn 6:16ff). During another violent storm at sea, the desperate disciples roused Jesus, who was sound asleep in the boat, begging him to save them. A complete calm ensued when he rebuked the winds and waves. His presence with them in the boat allayed all their fears (Mt 8:23ff).

We have experienced in some way how much a presence means at the time of death in a family. Martha and Mary found great comfort and consolation in the presence of Jesus when their beloved brother Lazarus died. Note, too, that before Jesus raised Lazarus to life again, he asked for faith. Martha convincingly responded: "Yes, Lord. I have come to believe that you are the Messiah, the Son of God, the one who is coming into the world" (Jn 11:27).

On the day of the resurrection, Jesus' appearance in the Upper Room, where the disciples had hidden themselves for fear of the Jews, brought great joy and a profound healing. These disciples were stricken with a painful sense of guilt since they abandoned Jesus in "his hour." Their anxieties, fears, and guilty feelings were replaced with great rejoicing as Jesus' forgiving presence touched them.

The Healer Forever

Does Jesus continue to heal us today? Jesus came into the world to be our Savior and healer. He is now in his glory, but what is his glory? His glory is the continuation of his redemptive mission among us. He wishes to fulfill the role of healer in our lives today because he knows that we will always be in need of his healing. Scripture tells us that "Jesus Christ is the same yesterday, today, and forever" (Heb 13:8).

Jesus desires to heal us in every area of our lives where we need his healing. There is, however, one important condition necessary before his healing power can be effective. First and foremost, we must have a deep faith and trust in his eagerness to heal us. We need only recall the many times in the Gospels when Jesus reminded the person who was healed that it was their faith which healed them. Many times God wants our response of faith before he will act. Our faith likewise must be an expectant faith. Our trust and confidence in his healing love must be strong and vibrant.

In the Gospels, when a person approached Jesus begging for a healing, he often asked: "Do you want to be healed?" That may seem like an irrelevant question. But Jesus wanted people to understand that if he healed them they might well have to change their lifestyle. Jesus wanted people to understand and to acknowledge that they were willing to change.

This second condition also applies to us. We must be open to whatever changes the Lord wants to effect in our life before he can heal us. We may have to give up something or someone we cherish. We must be willing to forgive and not harbor any desire of retaliation. There may be other hindrances which prevent a healing. The Lord will point these out to us when we come seeking his healing. Jesus says to each of us: "Do you want to be healed?"

The Healing Church

Since our broken human nature is so prone to sin, we are vulnerable to the pain and hurts which our own sinfulness and brokenness can cause us as well as the wounds another can inflict on us. Jesus was well aware that our weakened human nature would always stand in need of healing. That is why he established his church as a healing church. He instituted the sacramental life of the church to give us channels of healing in our lives.

The sacrament of baptism enables us to span that infinite chasm between the sinfulness of our human nature and the divine life which the Lord wishes to impart to us as the Holy Spirit comes to make his special dwelling place within us. Baptism gives us the potential to receive his indwelling presence. St. Paul asks us: "Do you not know that you are the temple of God, and that the Spirit of God dwells in you? If anyone destroys God's temple, God will destroy that person; for the temple of God, which you are, is holy" (1 Cor 3:16ff). Baptism is a divinely empowered channel of healing.

In his pastoral letter, the apostle James instructs us on the healing power of the sacrament of the anointing of the sick. Ponder his words: "Is anyone among you sick? He should summon the presbyters of the church, and they should pray over him and anoint [him] with oil in the name of the Lord, and the prayer of faith will save the sick person, and the Lord will raise him up" (Jas 5:14-15). There can be no doubt about the sacramental power of healing through this channel of grace.

The church points to the empowerment of the apostles to

forgive sins in the name of Jesus. This all occurred on the day of the resurrection after Jesus had repaired the fractured, fragmented relationship between God and mankind by his redemptive death on the cross. The evangelist John records this saving event in these words: " 'As the Father has sent me, so I send you.' And when he had said this, he breathed on them and said to them, 'Receive the Holy Spirit. Whose sins you forgive are forgiven them, and whose sins you retain are retained' " (Jn 20:21ff).

We also experience a great healing power embodied in the celebration of the Eucharist. Jesus is present in his Word and that Word has power to heal. Through the prophet Isaiah, the Lord assures us of the power of his word, comparing it to the rain and snow which water the earth. "So shall my word be that goes forth from my mouth; It shall not return to me void, but shall do my will, achieving the end for which I sent it" (Is 55:11). Jesus reminds us: "You are already pruned because of the word that I spoke to you" (Jn 15:3). As we expose our thinking and attitudes to the Word of God in the Liturgy of the Word at Mass, a conversion and transformation begins to take place within us. We discover that our mind and heart are not in tune with the heart and mind of Jesus. Yes, there is power in his Word.

Jesus is present in the Liturgy of the Eucharist also. There is a powerful healing in his eucharistic presence. We have all experienced a healing in a human presence when someone comes to visit us. It raises our spirits. There is a much greater healing power in the divine presence, especially when we receive the divine healer in Communion. This is one of the reasons why Jesus chose to remain with us sacramentally since he knew that we would be constantly in need of his healing love.

How to Use This Book

This book, entitled *Make Me Clean*, offers only thirty-one of the numerous healings recorded in the Word of God. For each day of the month one healing found in Scripture is presented along with a brief reflection which hopefully will stimulate your prayer of the heart.

In contemplating the healing mission of Jesus, enter into a prayer posture gradually and gently. Choose a comfortable, quiet place for your daily time of prayer. Having such a regular place for prayer will help you to relax into a listening frame of mind. Psychologists recommend an upright position with your feet on the floor as the most relaxed prayer posture.

Next, pause for a few moments to recollect yourself. Recall that the Lord is present with you and that it is he himself who is speaking to you through his Word.

After some time, read the scriptural passage slowly and reflectively. Permit every word to settle into your inner being. Continue your reading with the commentary which follows the words of Scripture.

Then begin to read the scriptural passage again. Ponder and rest on any word, phrase, expression, or thought which especially touches you. Remain in this resting place and savor the experience as long as your spirit enjoys the presence of the Lord. It is not necessary to complete the reading or the reflection on the whole passage again. Let the Lord lead you.

In this time spent savoring God's healing love, look beyond the words, the actions, the people involved, and the nature of the healing into the mind and heart of Jesus. Let these points of reference be like a window through which you behold divinity. Try to experience and feel the love and compassion which filled the heart of Jesus. Captivate his great desire to bring healing, relief, comfort, and peace and joy to the sufferer.

Conclude your prayer time by turning to Jesus. Thank and praise him for his healing love. Ask for his healing in some specific area of your life. Or maybe seek his healing in a general way for all the attitudes and feelings within you which are not in tune with his mindset, his attitude of healing love and compassion toward all.

The Fruits of This Approach

As we contemplate the many miraculous healings wrought by Jesus as recorded in the Gospels, we will enjoy a threefold fruit in our devotional life.

In the first place, our reflections should move us into a much greater spirit of gratitude. As we see Jesus reaching out in loving concern to anyone who comes to him in need of healing, we will naturally be moved to a more profound realization of the great compassion and love which filled the heart of Jesus. We will have a deeper insight into his divine personality. We will come to know him as a God who cares and is vitally concerned about us. Since we become what we contemplate, we will become more like Jesus even though we are not aware of it happening inside us.

Second, our time spent in meditating upon one of the scriptural accounts of a healing by Jesus will lead us into a greater spirit of compassion. We will better understand the great compassion which Jesus had for everyone he met and also the same compassion that he has for us. He willingly and eagerly suffered for us in order to redeem our sinful human nature. This realization will prompt us to a greater compassion for all who cross our path each day.

Third, we will begin to understand in a deeper way that the motivating force in all of Jesus' healing was his caring, concerned love. Jesus healed because he loved. He did not want any person to suffer physically, spiritually, or emotionally. His infinite love compelled him to heal. Our awareness of the boundless love of Jesus for us will empower us to respond to him in a more gracious and generous way. Love is mutual. Love begets love. As the gracious love of Jesus touches us, we will be impelled to fulfill that all-important law of love with which Jesus charged us: "Love your neighbor as yourself."

Our daily prayerful reflections on the healing love of the

Lord will increase our own confidence and trust not only in his power to heal, but also in his eagerness to heal. We will be encouraged to seek his healing in all the areas of our own life where we need his healing touch. More and more we will recognize how sensitive and fragile our human nature is and how badly we stand in need of his healing. We will become especially aware of the areas where we need an inner healing of our self-centeredness, our pride, our anger, and all the other barriers which stand in the way of putting on the mind and heart of the Lord.

With the leper may our prayer always be: "Lord, if you wish, you can make me clean." We can be assured that Jesus' reply will always be: "I do will it. Be made clean" (Lk 5:12-13).

ONE

Wash Seven Times

Naaman, the army commander of the king of Aram, was highly esteemed and respected by his master, for through him the LORD had brought victory to Aram. But valiant as he was, the man was a leper. Now the Arameans had captured from the land of Israel in a raid a little girl, who became the servant of Naaman's wife. "If only my master would present himself to the prophet in Samaria," she said to her mistress, "he would cure him of his leprosy." Naaman went and told his lord just what the slave girl from the land of Israel had said. "Go," said the king of Aram. "I will send along a letter to the king of Israel." So Naaman set out, taking along ten silver talents, six thousand gold pieces, and ten festal garments. To the king of Israel he brought the letter, which read: "With this letter I am sending my servant Naaman to you, that you may cure him of his leprosy."

When he read the letter, the king of Israel tore his garments and exclaimed: "Am I a god with power over life and death, that this man should send someone to me to be cured of leprosy? Take note! You can see he is only looking for a quarrel with me!" When Elisha, the man of God, heard that the king of Israel had torn his garments, he sent word to the king: "Why have you torn your garments? Let him come to me and find out that there is a prophet in Israel."

Naaman came with his horses and chariots and stopped at the door of Elisha's house. The prophet sent him the message: "Go and wash seven times in the Jordan, and your flesh will heal, and you will be clean." But Naaman went away angry, saying, "I thought that he would surely come out and stand there to invoke the LORD his God, and would move his hand over the spot, and thus cure the leprosy. Are not the rivers of Damascus, the Abana and the Pharpar, better than all the waters of Israel? Could I not wash in them and be cleansed?" With this, he turned about in anger and left.

But his servants came up and reasoned with him. "My father," they said, "if the prophet had told you to do something extraordinary, would you not have done it? All the more now, since he said to you, 'Wash and be clean,' should you do as he said." So Naaman went down and plunged into the Jordan seven times at the word of the man of God. His flesh became again like the flesh of a little child, and he was clean.

He returned with his whole retinue to the man of God. On his arrival he stood before him and said, "Now I know that there is no God in all the earth, except in Israel. Please accept a gift from your servant."

"As the LORD lives whom I serve, I will not take it," Elisha replied; and despite Naaman's urging, he still refused. Naaman said: "If you will not accept, please let me, your servant, have two mule-loads of earth, for I will no longer offer holocaust or sacrifice to any other god except to the LORD." (2 Kgs 5:1-17)

A half-dozen high school students invited me to an evening of entertainment at their school. The program consisted of three one-act plays based on some scriptural account. My six friends were the entire cast for the last one-act play of the evening. They dramatized the healing of Naaman as recorded in 2 Kings 5:1-19.

I have often reflected not only on their presentation of the healing of Naaman, but also on the powerful healing presence of the Lord when faith is manifested. The Lord extended his healing love to Naaman even though he was a pagan. I thought of all the "personae dramatis" which God had arranged to bring about this remarkable healing.

The "little girl, who became the servant of Naaman's wife" did not understand why she was taken into captivity. In this distant land, she must have missed her family and friends. Yet God had plans for her. Were it not for her presence and her faith, Naaman might never have been cured. She initiated the healing process when she said to her mistress: "If only my master would present himself to the prophet in Samaria he would cure him of his leprosy." Like this little girl, we, too, play a similar role in God's divine design. We may never be aware of how God is using us. It calls for a faith and trust on our part and also a willing mind and heart to respond to whatever the Lord may ask of us.

The servants also played a vital role in this healing drama. These servants, too, were chosen and used by God. Their faith was sufficient to encourage their master Naaman to heed the directive of Elisha. It was their persuasive reasoning that finally convinced Naaman. "So Naaman went down and plunged into the Jordan seven times at the word of the man of God."

The wife of Naaman had confidence in the words of the servant girl. She loved her husband and wanted him to try every available means to be cured. The seed of faith was beginning to germinate in her heart.

Elisha's prophetic words were also based on his own faith in the Lord. His faith was one of expectancy, knowing that the Lord would hear and respond to their common prayer.

However, when Naaman "stopped at the door of Elisha's house" and received the message to go and wash seven times in the river Jordan, he rebelled because his faith was not yet strong enough to accept God's ways. This humiliating test challenged Naaman's faith. He was so angered that he almost flunked the test. Such a procedure seemed inane and ridiculous to him. How could ordinary river water heal the dreadful disease of leprosy? he thought with pride in his heart.

Listening to the persuasive words of his servants, Naaman's faith was rewarded. "His flesh became again like the flesh of a little child, and he was clean." Faith is the first and foremost requisite for the Lord's healing. As we contemplate this episode in Scripture, we will notice that every person involved in this drama had varying degrees of faith. The development of Naaman's faith should give us hope and encouragement for our own lives.

The seed of faith in Naaman's heart began to germinate when he heard of the prophet's ministry. The supportive words of his wife watered that seedling of faith. Naaman's faith of commitment began when he set out on the journey to Elisha's home. As his faith was tested, it grew stronger, and it finally blossomed into the faith of commitment. "Now I know that there is no God in all the earth, except in Israel," he testified after his healing. We, too, are called to that kind of faith. Furthermore, we are also called to strengthen the faith of others by word and example, letting God use even our own meager faith to reach others with his love.

TWO

I Can See

When they had finished eating and drinking, the girl's parents wanted to retire. They brought the young man out of the dining room and led him into the bedroom. At this point Tobiah, mindful of Raphael's instructions, took the fish's liver and heart from the bag which he had with him, and placed them on the embers for the incense. The demon, repelled by the odor of the fish, fled into Upper Egypt; Raphael pursued him there and bound him hand and foot. Then Raphael returned immediately.

When the girl's parents left the bedroom and closed the door behind them, Tobiah arose from bed and said to his wife, "My love, get up. Let us pray and beg our Lord to have mercy on us and grant us deliverance." She got up, and they started to pray and beg that deliverance might be theirs. He began with these words:

"Blessed are you, O God of our fathers;
praised be your name forever and ever.
Let the heavens and all your creation
praise you forever.
You made Adam and you gave him his wife Eve
to be his help and support;
and from these two the human race descended.

You said, 'It is not good for the man to be alone;
let us make him a partner like himself.'
Now, Lord, you know that I take this wife of mine
not because of lust,
but for a noble purpose.
Call down your mercy on me and on her,
and allow us to live together to a happy old age."
They said together, "Amen, amen," and went to bed for the
night. . . . (Tb 8:1-8)

Tobiah went up to him with the fish gall in his hand, and
holding him firmly, blew into his eyes. "Courage, father," he
said. Next he smeared the medicine on his eyes, and it made
them smart. Then, beginning at the corners of Tobit's eyes,
Tobiah used both hands to peel off the cataracts. When
Tobit saw his son, he threw his arms around him and wept.
He exclaimed, "I can see you, son, the light of my eyes!"
Then he said:

"Blessed be God,
and praised be his great name,
and blessed be all his holy angels.
May his holy name be praised
throughout all the ages,
Because it was he who scourged me,
and it is he who has had mercy on me.
Behold, I now see my son Tobiah!
Then Tobit went back in, rejoicing and praising God with
full voice. Tobiah told his father that his journey had been
a success; that he had brought back the money; and that
he had married Raguel's daughter Sarah, who would
arrive shortly, for she was approaching the gate of
Nineveh. (Tb 11:10-15)

In the Book of Tobit we have an account of two marvelous
healings by the Lord. Just as God sent his angel Raphael to
manifest his healing power to young Tobiah and to his blind

father Tobit, so he wants to heal our own blindness, which may be a spiritual or emotional blindness that hinders us from serving the Lord.

The Book of Tobit is a fascinating story of God's caring, concerned love for every person especially for those who live his way of life. Tobit was such a man. He walked in the way of the Lord all his life. He was a devout and faithful Hebrew even in the land of exile. At the risk of his own life, he buried his dead brothers and sisters who were slain by their captors. This act was forbidden under pain of death, but Tobit respected and loved God more than men.

We can readily understand why God showered his blessings upon Tobit and his family. In the first place Tobit obeyed the laws of God in every detail.

Second, young Tobiah followed precisely the instructions which Raphael had given. "At this point Tobiah, mindful of Raphael's instructions, took the fish's liver and heart from the bag which he had with him, and placed them on the embers for the incense. The demon, repelled by the odor of the fish, fled into Upper Egypt" (Tb 8:2-3). The Lord's healing power broke the grip of the evil one.

On his return home, young Tobiah again followed exactly the instructions of Raphael by applying the fish gall to his father's eyes. This procedure might have seemed a bit foolish to Tobiah, but he faithfully obeyed the commands given him. Before their very eyes God's healing power was again manifest. The Lord miraculously restored Tobit's vision.

This touching story moves us to pause and reflect on our own docility, our own responsiveness to the inspirations and directions of the Lord. We need healing spiritually, psychologically, and physically many times, but we must step out in faith and trust by confidently asking the Lord to grant us such blessings. We must believe that God is willing and eager to extend his healing love to us if we believe and trust in him at the very depth of our being. Recall that the Gospels tell us that on several occasions Jesus could not perform any miracles in certain places because of their lack of faith.

Our trust in God also helps us to accept some affliction. In the case of Tobit, his blindness was temporary. God permitted Tobit's blindness in order to manifest his healing power at the appropriate time, according to his plans. God may do the same in our lives.

God is constantly healing us even though we may not be aware of it. He may heal us so that we can overcome bitterness and anger. He may remove obstacles to his work within us so he can increase our faith and trust. He may heal us of the problems which prevent us from entering into a deeper, more personal relationship with him through prayer. We may never know just how often and how much God has healed us.

THREE

He Heals All Your Ills

Bless the LORD, O my soul;
  and all my being, bless his holy name.
Bless the LORD, O my soul,
  and forget not all his benefits;
He pardons all your iniquities,
  he heals all your ills.
He redeems your life from destruction,
  he crowns you with kindness and compassion,
He fills your lifetime with good;
  your youth is renewed like the eagle's.
The LORD secures justice
  and the rights of all the oppressed.
He has made known his ways to Moses,
  and his deeds to the children of Israel.
Merciful and gracious is the LORD,
  slow to anger and abounding in kindness.
He will not always chide,
  nor does he keep his wrath forever.
Not according to our sins does he deal with us,
  nor does he requite us according to our crimes.
For as the heavens are high above the earth,
  so surpassing is his kindness toward

those who fear him.
As far as the east is from the west,
   so far has he put our transgressions from us.
As a father has compassion on his children,
   so the LORD has compassion on those who fear him,
For he knows how we are formed;
   he remembers that we are dust.
Man's days are like those of grass;
   like a flower of the field he blooms;
The wind sweeps over him and he is gone,
   and his place knows him no more.
But the kindness of the LORD is from eternity
   to eternity toward those who fear him,
And his justice toward children's children
      among those who keep his covenant
      and remember to fulfill his precepts. (Ps 103:1-18)

For several years I enjoyed the privilege of leading long retreats in Tiberias, Israel for religious orders of sisters that serve in Third World countries. During one of my sojourns I befriended an elderly Jewish rabbi. Together we talked often about the Hebrew Testament, especially about the Psalms.

He explained to me that our approach to the Psalms is usually opposite that of the author. When we pray the Psalms we listen with our whole being to the words, hoping that they will lead us into a contemplative awareness of God's goodness and love, of his mercy and compassion.

On the other hand, the psalmist first had an experience of God's might and majesty, of his loving care and concern. Only after the experience did the psalmist strive to express in lyrical form his encounter with the Lord. It was time for the rabbi to catch his bus. His parting words to me were: "Pray Psalm 103." I did so immediately.

In this Psalm the writer realized more fully the tremendous healing power of God. After the psalmist had experienced the

Lord's healing power, he tried to express his wonder and awe in these words:

> He pardons all your iniquities,
>   he heals all your ills.
> He redeems your life from destruction,
>   he crowns you with kindness and compassion. (vv. 3-4)

God is our healer. He wants to heal us more than we want it for ourselves. We can be certain of this truth because his love for us is infinite and a person must give in proportion to the intensity of his love. The Lord helps us by pardoning our offenses and showering his mercy and compassion upon us. We must first recognize our sinfulness and our need for forgiveness and healing. Then we must be open to receive his healing as we implore his mercy and compassion.

A total healing depends on yet another all-important condition. We must be willing to forgive anyone who might have hurt us. Jesus' words are quite direct and imperative. "If you forgive others their transgressions, your heavenly Father will forgive you. But if you do not forgive others, neither will your Father forgive your transgressions" (Mt 6:14-15).

The psalmist said that he enjoyed the constant and continuing beneficence of the Lord which he tried to summarize in song: "He fills your lifetime with good; your youth is renewed like the eagle's" (v. 5). The image of an eagle is a very apt one. It is highly symbolic. The life span of an eagle is very long, some even live a hundred years. This image conveys the perpetual goodness and healing of the Lord throughout our lifetime.

There is another symbolic significance to this image. After an eagle molts, his strength and vigor return to him. After the Lord heals us, we, too, are invigorated and filled with peace and joy. Such a healing disposes us to renew our devotion and dedication to God with greater intensity.

When we ponder the merciful forgiveness and healing of the

Lord, we are moved to a spirit of praise and gratitude. In our prayer may our hearts, bursting with praise and thankfulness, soar like the eagle to great heights as we exclaim:

> Bless the LORD, O my soul;
>> and all my being, bless his holy name.
> Bless the LORD, O my soul,
>> and forget not all his benefits. (vv. 1-2)

FOUR

If You Forgive Others

"This is how you are to pray:
  Our Father in heaven,
  hallowed be your name,
  your kingdom come,
  your will be done,
  on earth as in heaven.
  Give us today our daily bread;
  and forgive us our debts,
  as we forgive our debtors;
  and do not subject us to the final test,
  but deliver us from the evil one.
  If you forgive others their transgressions, your heavenly
Father will forgive you. But if you do not forgive others,
neither will your Father forgive your transgressions." (Mt
6:9-15)

One of St. Maria Goretti's biographers tells us that the
young man who murdered her was released from prison on
Christmas Eve. Immediately after the prison gates closed
behind him, he went directly to the home of the mother of
Maria Goretti to ask her to forgive him for the terrible crime he
had committed. Maria's mother forgave him and together they
went to Midnight Mass. This good mother was trying to live

out the Lord's Prayer in her life. Countless times she prayed: "Forgive us our trespasses as we forgive those who trespass against us." Now she was striving to put these words into practice.

The greatest healing which all of us need is forgiveness for our sinfulness. Jesus' instruction to us is clear and direct: "If you forgive others their transgressions, your heavenly Father will forgive you. But if you do not forgive others, neither will your Father forgive your transgressions" (v. 14-15). Most of us find forgiveness rather difficult. When we have been wronged or hurt, the wound does not easily heal, nor is it easy to forget. The Lord knows how hard it is at times for us to forgive. That is why he is most concerned with our intention. If we want to forgive, if in our humanness we make an honest effort to forgive, the Lord will accept that as forgiveness. If we could forgive totally and completely, it would be a special gift from our loving Father.

Jesus gives us such powerful examples of forgiveness in his own life. When the crowd came to arrest him in the Garden of Gethsemane, Peter in his impetuosity tried to defend Jesus with his sword. All he accomplished was to cut off the ear of the high priest's servant. Jesus' reaction was truly divine as he commanded: " 'Stop, no more of this!' Then he touched the servant's ear and healed him" (Lk 22:51ff). Jesus' reaction is indeed a compelling and challenging example for us. In his Sermon on the Mount, Jesus said: "Love your enemies, and pray for those who persecute you" (Mt 5:44). Jesus transferred this teaching into action as he healed the high priest's servant.

In that same discourse Jesus tells us how very important it is for us not only to forgive others, but also to ask for forgiveness if we have wronged anyone. "If you bring your gift to the altar, and there recall that your brother has anything against you, leave your gift there at the altar, go first and be reconciled with your brother, and then come and offer your gift" (Mt 5:23f). Jesus gave us a striking example when he offered the gift of himself on the altar of the cross. His merciful compassion and forgiveness reached a tremendous climax on Calvary's hill. He not only prayed for his enemies, he also excused them. ["Father, forgive them, they know not what they do"] (Lk 23:34).

When we find it difficult, or almost impossible, to forgive another person, we would do well to climb the hill of Calvary in spirit to stand under the cross of Jesus. We may have to linger there for considerable time until we begin to comprehend what is taking place. As we listen to the blasphemy, the insults, and the derision leveled at the transcendent God of heaven and earth, we begin to realize that our own sinfulness has contributed to this infamous rejection of the very Son of God. As these thoughts move from our mind to our heart, we will find it easier to say, "I forgive."

FIVE

Yes, Lord

And as Jesus passed on from there, two blind men followed [him], crying out, "Son of David, have pity on us!" When he entered the house, the blind men approached him and Jesus said to them, "Do you believe that I can do this?" "Yes, Lord," they said to him. Then he touched their eyes and said, "Let it be done for you according to your faith." And their eyes were opened. Jesus warned them sternly, "See that no one knows about this." But they went out and spread word of him through all that land. (Mt 9:27-31)

During his public ministry Jesus frequently encountered blindness. It is a distressingly common disease in the Near East. It is caused by the glare of the Eastern sun on unprotected eyes and also by a lack of hygiene and cleanliness.

When the two blind men cried out to Jesus, he did not respond to them immediately. Perhaps, they might have been swayed by the enthusiasm of the crowd which always followed Jesus. They may not have been sincere or in earnest in crying out to Jesus for a healing. Jesus wanted to determine their sincerity. He wanted to test their faith.

These two men were beggars. In Israel not everyone could beg. Only professional beggars who had some kind of handicap were permitted to solicit help. There was some advantage to being a beggar. You did not have to assume the responsibility of making a living.

When we are in need of healing and appeal to Jesus for his healing touch, we, too, must be sincere in asking for a healing. It is possible that we may not want to give up certain habits of sinfulness, or change our way of living, or be more diligent in fulfilling certain duties. We need to examine our real motives when we ask Jesus to heal us. Is our faith sincere?

Jesus wanted to ascertain if these men really had enough faith to be healed. He asked only one question: "Do you believe that I can do this?" When they responded affirmatively, Jesus said: "Let it be done for you according to your faith." Faith is always a necessary condition for receiving a healing. We, too, must approach Jesus with a strong faith of expectancy.

After Jesus restored their sight, he "warned them sternly" not to tell anyone about the healing. Jesus healed because he loved and not simply to demonstrate his divine power. Jesus wanted people to come to him because they believed in him, not simply to receive a healing or some other benefit.

The steps by which Jesus led these blind men to be receptive to his healing power can also guide us in preparing to receive his healing in our daily lives. We need to be sincere and detached from anything which might prevent us from forming a deep personal relationship with Jesus. We need that vibrant, operative faith which keeps us aware that Jesus is always with us and will help us if we are open and receptive to his divine power and love. When Jesus asks us: "Do you believe that I can do this?" may our response always be "Yes, Lord."

SIX

Come to Me

"Come to me, all you who labor and are burdened, and I will give you rest. Take my yoke upon you and learn from me, for I am meek and humble of heart; and you will find rest for yourselves. For my yoke is easy, and my burden light." (Mt 11:28-30)

". . . And behold, I am with you always, until the end of the age." (Mt 28:20)

"I will not leave you orphans; I will come to you." (Jn 14:18)

I was visiting my friend Ann in a retirement home. Aware that many older people experience a great deal of loneliness after having lived an active life, I asked Ann a rather naive question: "Do you get lonely at times?"

Her answer was refreshing. She paused for a moment and then said: "No, not really. My son and daughter are faithful in visiting me, and my daughter calls me almost daily. Every time my daughter leaves me, she uses the same farewell: The Lord be with you and keep you, Mom." Ann continued: "There are so many things to talk over with the Lord. I wonder sometimes if he gets bored with me because I thank him for many things which happened long years ago. I tell him all about my children and grandchildren. We have some pretty good conversations."

Ann's dialogue with the Lord is not empty or futile sharing. It springs from her deep personal relationship with the Lord. It is her prayer life. Ann was right. She was not lonely because there is much healing in God's abiding presence. We discover that on a human level as well. A visit from a friend or family member whose company we enjoy brings peace and happiness to us. There is much comfort and consolation in knowing that we are loved, accepted, and appreciated by someone.

If we are feeling a bit down, or discouraged, or lonely, a visit from someone dear to us can bring great healing. We know that someone cares. Someone is concerned enough to come and be with us. Even a brief period of time approached this way can be a healing time.

If there is healing in a human presence when we are in need, how much greater healing comes through God's saving presence. Jesus was well aware that we would need to experience his closeness to us. This is why he gave us the reassurance: "And behold, I am with you always, until the end of the age" (Mt 28:20). In fact, the presence of the Lord was prophesied and promised eight hundred years before the birth of Jesus. Isaiah foretold: "The virgin shall be with child, and bear a son, and shall name him Immanuel" (Is 7:14). In his Gospel, Matthew reminds us of the fidelity of the Lord to his promise: "... and they shall name him Emmanuel, which means 'God is with us' " (Mt 1:23).

Jesus came into the world to be our Savior, our Redeemer and healer. He has now entered into his glory. But what is his glory? His glory is to continue his healing mission among us. Scripture reminds us that "Jesus Christ is the same yesterday, today, and forever" (Heb 13:8). Jesus is pleased when we recall his presence among us, when we recognize his ongoing healing mission in our midst. There can be no doubt that his presence is a healing presence, as he shares his love, his peace, and his joy with us.

If we are disheartened or discouraged, if we are not feeling well, if we are giving in to self-pity, or if we have been hurt or insulted, a brief pause to recall the presence of the Lord will be a soothing balm to our woundedness. We may even at times imagine the Lord is putting his arm around us and telling us that we are very much like him as we accept the little pin-pricks and jabs that come our way in everyday life.

As the sun brightens and warms up the day, so does God's love nurture and heal us as we bask in his healing and abiding presence. Jesus knows that we need his healing presence; hence, he continually invites us:

"Come to me, all you who labor and are burdened, and I will give you rest." (Mt 11:28)

SEVEN

Your Sins Are Forgiven

When Jesus returned to Capernaum after some days, it became known that he was at home. Many gathered together so that there was no longer room for them, not even around the door, and he preached the word to them. They came bringing to him a paralytic carried by four men. Unable to get near Jesus because of the crowd, they opened up the roof above him. After they had broken through, they let down the mat on which the paralytic was lying. When Jesus saw their faith, he said to the paralytic, "Child, your sins are forgiven."

Now some of the scribes were sitting there asking themselves, "Why does this man speak that way? He is blaspheming. Who but God alone can forgive sins?" Jesus immediately knew in his mind what they were thinking to themselves, so he said, "Why are you thinking such things in your hearts? Which is easier, to say to the paralytic, 'Your sins are forgiven,' or to say, 'Rise, pick up your mat and walk'? But that you may know that the Son of Man has authority to forgive sins on earth"—he said to the paralytic, "I say to you, rise, pick up your mat, and go home." He rose, picked up his mat at once, and went away in the sight of everyone. They were all astounded and glorified God, saying, "We have never seen anything like this." (Mk 2:1-12)

I was watching a pro-football game on television with Tom, a good friend of mine. He carefully analyzed every play, always pointing out the importance of teamwork. During the game whenever a key player was able to do his special task well, the team made great progress. Tom kept reminding me that it all depended on teamwork. I respected his opinion since he is a high school football coach. His motto is: "Good teamwork produces a winning team."

Jesus endorsed much the same view when he showed how pleased he was with the team of four men who carried the paralyzed man on a litter to him for a healing. This endeavor required teamwork. When they arrived at the place where Jesus was teaching, they could not bring the paralytic to him because of the huge crowd surrounding him. They proved their resourcefulness and their faith.

The homes in Israel at the time of Jesus were very small. People spent a great deal of time on their flat rooftops, which were usually quite accessible. It was probably from here that the men let down the paralytic in front of Jesus.

At any rate, Jesus was very pleased with their teamwork. He admired not only their ingenuity and perseverance, but their deep faith in making every effort to bring the paralyzed man to him. Their faith did not go unnoticed. Jesus was pleased with the strong faith of this little community. Those men who carried the paralytic really believed that Jesus had the power to heal. The evangelist Mark is careful to note that "when Jesus saw their faith, he said to the paralytic, 'Child, your sins are forgiven.'" Surely the faith of the team who carried the man to him impressed Jesus. Perhaps next to Jesus' great healing love, their faith was the motivating factor in bringing about this wonderful healing.

This team brought the man to Jesus to be healed of his paralysis, but Jesus always healed the whole person—body, soul, and spirit. Jesus was compelled to heal the whole person because his love is without limit and that kind of love cannot be satisfied until it gives all that it can. Jesus was under close scrutiny, but that did not deter him in any way. The reaction of the scribes who dogged Jesus' footsteps was not unexpected. They accused Jesus of blasphemy because he forgave sins. For they knew that kind of power and authority belonged to God alone. Jesus took the occasion not only to prove his divine power to forgive sins and to heal souls as well as bodies. No, he also demonstrated his fathomless love in restoring to health the whole person—physically, psychologically, emotionally, and spiritually.

How clearly and emphatically he stated it when he said: " 'That you may know that the Son of Man has authority to forgive sins on earth'—he said to the paralytic, 'I say to you, rise, pick up your mat, and go home.' He rose, picked up his mat at once, and went away in the sight of everyone." Jesus continues his redemptive ministry of forgiving sins in the sacrament of reconciliation. There he eagerly awaits our encounter with him that he might assure us: "Your sins are forgiven."

We see in this passage, then, that the Lord is deeply moved by the faith of a community when that community comes to him seeking healing. The community may be a family in need of healing. It may be a religious community, a parish, or an organization of some sort. The key is that the members come to the Lord in faith and trust seeking a healing of relationships. Such community-based faith can be a powerful healing force for those in need.

Let us join the witnesses to the healing of the paralytic in praising and glorifying our compassionate God for his healing love. And let us decide to seek God's healing for those in our own midst, in our families and in our parish communities.

EIGHT

Legion Is My Name

They came to the other side of the sea, to the territory of the Gerasenes. When he got out of the boat, at once a man from the tombs who had an unclean spirit met him. The man had been dwelling among the tombs, and no one could restrain him any longer, even with a chain. In fact, he had frequently been bound with shackles and chains, but the chains had been pulled apart by him and the shackles smashed, and no one was strong enough to subdue him. Night and day among the tombs and on the hillsides he was always crying out and bruising himself with stones. Catching sight of Jesus from a distance, he ran up and prostrated himself before him, crying out in a loud voice, "What have you to do with me, Jesus, Son of the Most High God? I adjure you by God, do not torment me!" (He had been saying to him, "Unclean spirit, come out of the man!") He asked him, "What is your name?" He replied, "Legion is my name. There are many of us." And he pleaded earnestly with him not to drive them away from that territory.

Now a large herd of swine was feeding there on the hillside. And they pleaded with him, "Send us into the swine. Let us enter them." And he let them, and the unclean spirits came out and entered the swine. The herd of about two thousand rushed down a steep bank into the sea, where they were drowned. The swineherds ran away and reported the incident in the town and throughout the countryside. And people came out to see what had happened. As they approached Jesus, they caught sight of the man who had been possessed by Legion, sitting there clothed and in his right mind. And they were seized with fear. Those who witnessed the incident explained to them what had happened to the possessed man and to the swine. Then they began to beg him to leave their district. As he was getting into the boat, the man who had been possessed pleaded to remain with him. But he would not permit him but told him instead, "Go home to your family and announce to them all that the Lord in his pity has done for you." Then the man went off and began to proclaim in the Decapolis what Jesus had done for him; and all were amazed. (Mk 5:1-20)

During a talk I attended on discernment of spirits, the speaker was explaining that temptations can arise frequently as we try to enter more deeply into prayer. He spoke about the subtlety of the evil spirit. He insisted that the devil is extremely cunning and clever in getting us worried, anxious, doubting, and impatient about our relationship with the Lord. He also mentioned that the devil is delighted when some people try to deny his very existence. That gives him an arena where he can operate unmolested.

The episode in Scripture which we are contemplating today has all the earmarks of real possession by an evil, unclean spirit. We meet Jesus as he disembarks from the boat which brought him to the east shore of the Sea of Galilee and into the land of the Gerasenes. We walk along with him and sense how eager he was to bring the message of the good news to these gentiles who perhaps had little or no knowledge of the one true God.

As we walk along with Jesus in this Gerasene territory, we hear a sudden piercing and shrieking cry rend the air. It is a cry of desperation coming from a man who is possessed by the devil. It is quite apparent that an unclean spirit is present in this poor man. This man has lived in the tombs. He cannot be restrained by either chains or shackles.

Picture for a moment the desperate sight which confronted Jesus. The man was naked. His entire countenance reflected a demented and tormented mind which the devil had robbed of its freedom. Try to get a sense of how this hideous sight and diabolical shrieking wrung the heart of Jesus.

The evil spirit within the demented man cried out: "What have you to do with me, Jesus, Son of the Most High God? I adjure you by God, do not torment me!"

Try for a moment to experience the feelings which must have filled the heart of Jesus. See the distress of this man through the eyes of Jesus. Feel the yearning within the heart of Jesus to rid this person of such dreadful suffering.

In his loving concern and deep compassion, Jesus reached out to this man who was in such desperate need of healing. The mind of the man had been deeply wounded. The man needed adequate proof in his confused state of mind to show that the devils were really driven out, never to bother him again. Jesus allowed the devils to enter into the herd of swine. In the sight of everyone: "The herd of about two thousand rushed down a steep bank into the sea, where they drowned." This demonstration left no doubt in the man's mind that he was freed of this diabolical influence. This public manifestation restored sanity to the man's mind. He found peace and joy once again. Jesus likewise accommodates himself to our needs. He may permit our faith to be tried at times, but he comes to our rescue to prove beyond any shadow of a doubt his loving care and concern.

The reaction of the people in this district may surprise us. When they saw this demonstration of divine power, you would expect them to welcome Jesus. On the contrary, their reaction was the opposite of this. "Then they began to beg him to leave their district." They regarded this happening with horror. They were afraid that Jesus might disturb their complacency.

We may find ourselves in a similar frame of mind. We may be

unwilling to ask the Lord for a healing, or even resist one because it might disturb our way of living. Like the Gerasenes, we may be stifling the inspiration and motivation of the Holy Spirit. How much greater would be our peace and happiness if we, like the healed man, would ask the Lord for a healing and then go off to proclaim what Jesus has done for us.

NINE

Take Nothing for the Journey

He went around to the villages in the vicinity teaching. He summoned the Twelve and began to send them out two by two and gave them authority over unclean spirits. He instructed them to take nothing for the journey but a walking stick—no food, no sack, no money in their belts. They were, however, to wear sandals but not a second tunic. He said to them, "Wherever you enter a house, stay there until you leave from there. Whatever place does not welcome you or listen to you, leave there and shake the dust off your feet in testimony against them." So they went off and preached repentance. They drove out many demons, and they anointed with oil many who were sick and cured them.

The apostles gathered together with Jesus and reported all they had done and taught. He said to them, "Come away by yourselves to a deserted place and rest a while." People were coming and going in great numbers, and they had no opportunity even to eat. (Mk 6:6-13, 30-31)

In the days of the great monasteries in Europe, people flocked to the monastery nearby to beg the monks to teach them how to pray. The hours of prayer and the physical work which the monks were required to perform, gave them little time to meet the needs of these good people. Furthermore, many of the people were unable to leave home to come to the monastery for instruction. To meet this need the monks trained monastic brothers in various forms of prayer and then sent them out to teach and instruct the people how to pray.

Jesus found himself in the same quandary. He came into the world to proclaim the good news of salvation and also to manifest his Father's love as well as his own. To accomplish this purpose, Jesus began his healing ministry by healing all who came to him with needs. The task was colossal. To meet the many needs of the people, he empowered his apostles and sent them out to expand his healing mission. "He summoned the Twelve and began to send them out two by two and gave them authority over unclean spirits." He instructed them to take only the bare essentials with them as they traveled along. This was to show their total dependence upon God. They could claim none of the power as their own.

When the apostles returned, they were thrilled with their success. It was then that Jesus advised them: "Come away by yourselves to a deserted place and rest a while." The purpose Jesus had in mind was to give the apostles quiet time to reflect on what God had accomplished through them. They were not to take any of the credit themselves.

Furthermore, Jesus wanted to prepare them to continue his healing mission after his return to the Father. After the ascension of Jesus into heaven, we find Peter and John encountering a cripple at the Beautiful Gate of the temple begging for alms (Acts 3:1-10). Peter responded to his request with: "I have neither silver nor gold, but what I do have I give you: in the name of Jesus Christ the Nazorean, [rise and] walk" (Acts 3:6). The healing power of the Lord flowed through the apostles. As Luke writes: "He leaped up, stood, and walked around, and went into the temple with them, walking and jumping and praising God" (Acts 3:8). Like the apostles we, too, are called by the Lord to be the instruments of his healing love. As temples of the Holy Spirit, the Lord is dynamic and operative within us. Today as always, there is great need for healing, especially for inner healing. Jesus is counting on us to channel his healing love and concern to others in need.

We can heal by our presence. It might be a visit to a lonely person, a cheerful smile to a passerby, or simply a healing touch.

We can heal by our words. It might be a well-deserved compliment, a sincere thank you, a word of acceptance, an expression of loving concern, a show of personal interest, or a word of comfort and consolation to someone in sorrow.

We can heal by our actions. It might be our attentive listening, a warm embrace, or a helping hand to meet some practical need.

Just as the divine healer empowered and commissioned the apostles to minister his healing love, to be channels of that love to others, so he asks us to be the instruments of his healing also. Speaking about the call to minister healing to others Jesus said: "Without cost you have received; without cost you are to give" (Mt 10:8). That is a call for each of us today.

TEN

I Do Believe

When they came to the disciples, they saw a large crowd around them and scribes arguing with them. Immediately on seeing him, the whole crowd was utterly amazed. They ran up to him and greeted him. He asked them, "What are you arguing about with them?" Someone from the crowd answered him, "Teacher, I have brought to you my son possessed by a mute spirit. Wherever it seizes him, it throws him down; he foams at the mouth, grinds his teeth, and becomes rigid. I asked your disciples to drive it out, but they were unable to do so." He said to them in reply, "O faithless generation, how long will I be with you? How long will I endure you? Bring him to me." They brought the boy to him. And when he saw him, the spirit immediately threw the boy into convulsions. As he fell to the ground, he began to roll around and foam at the mouth. Then he questioned his father, "How long has this been happening to him?" He replied, "Since childhood. It has often thrown him into fire and into water to kill him. But if you can do anything, have compassion on us and help us." Jesus said to him, " 'If you can!' Everything is possible to one who has faith." Then the boy's father cried out, "I do believe, help my unbelief!" Jesus, on seeing a crowd rapidly gathering, rebuked the unclean spirit and said to it, "Mute and deaf spirit, I command you: come out of him and never enter him again!" Shouting and throwing the boy into convulsions, it came out. He became like a corpse, which caused many to say, "He is dead!" But Jesus took him by the hand, raised him, and he stood up. When he entered the house, his disciples asked him in private, "Why could we not drive it out?" He said to them, "This kind can only come out through prayer." (Mk 9:14-29)

I have some vivid memories of one occasion when I was still a preschooler. My grandmother took me with her to Sunday Mass. The homily for that Mass was about the joys and bliss of heaven and how our time would be spent in praising and glorifying God for all eternity.

On our way home after Mass, my grandmother thought it important for the good of my soul to reemphasize all that the priest had said. I suppose I did not show much enthusiasm which caused my grandmother to ask why I did not seem more excited about the prospects of heaven. In response to her question I asked: "Grandmother, if I am a good boy and if I do go to heaven, do you think that Jesus will let me go out to play with the little devils sometimes?" Well, you can imagine my grandmother's reaction to my childish naivete!

It seems to me that Jesus must have had a similar experience in this episode immediately after the transfiguration. On Mount Tabor Jesus had just said "yes" to the Father. He would be willing to sacrifice his life for the redemption of the world. When he made this commitment he was transfigured before the very eyes of his three disciples. His divine splendor radiated through his whole being. As he came down from Mount Tabor, he was confronted with great disappointment in the lack of faith and trust on the part of his disciples. He was also challenged by the demon of epilepsy. How disappointed Jesus must have been to discover that his disciples whom he had chosen to proclaim the good news were beaten and baffled, helpless and unable to cure this tormented boy. The situation wrung a plaintive cry from the heart of Jesus: "O faithless generation, how long will I be with you? How long will I endure you?"

My grandmother must have felt the same frustration at my shortsightedness in moving from the lofty and heavenly thoughts of the homilist to my childish and earthly question. In reality it, too, was a step from the sublime and the heavenly to the ridiculous and the narrowly human concerns of this world.

The father of the boy now turned to Jesus in desperation and pleaded: "If you can do anything, have compassion on us and help us." This brought an exclamation from Jesus: " 'If you can!' Everything is possible to one who has faith." Jesus was telling the father that the healing depended upon his own faith. Jesus wanted to see an attitude of faith on the father's part before he would act. The father's faith was already badly shaken. He had lost confidence in the disciples when they failed in their attempt to cure his son. No wonder that he said to Jesus; "If you can do anything . . ." The father of the boy finally turned to Jesus with a prayer and a profession of faith. "I do believe, help my unbelief."

Jesus then took command: "Mute and deaf spirit, I command you: come out of him and never enter him again!" The spirit tried to resist, but was helpless against the divine command of Jesus. When the disciples later asked Jesus: "Why could we not drive it out?" He said to them: "This kind can only come out through prayer." Jesus used this occasion to teach us some valuable lessons. Prayer and faith go hand in hand. Our trust and confidence is deepened by prayer. The more fervently we pray the stronger will be our faith. Even in the most desperate moments when prayer and trust seem useless, Jesus invites his followers to go one step further and pray like the boy's father.

In almost all the healing situations in the Gospels, faith is always on the lips of Jesus as he uses his divine power to heal. For instance, he tells us: "Do not be afraid. Just have faith" (Mk 5:36). We must have the complete trust of little children who trust so implicitly in their parents' love that there is no room for doubt. May our prayer always be: "I do believe, help my unbelief."

ELEVEN

I Want to See

They came to Jericho. And as he was leaving Jericho with his
disciples and a sizable crowd, Bartimaeus, a blind man, the
son of Timaeus, sat by the roadside begging. On hearing
that it was Jesus of Nazareth, he began to cry out and say,
"Jesus, son of David, have pity on me." And many rebuked
him, telling him to be silent. But he kept calling out all the
more, "Son of David, have pity on me." Jesus stopped and
said, "Call him." So they called the blind man, saying to him,
"Take courage; get up, he is calling you." He threw aside his
cloak, sprang up, and came to Jesus. Jesus said to him in
reply, "What do you want me to do for you?" The blind man
replied to him, "Master, I want to see." Jesus told him, "Go
your way; your faith has saved you." Immediately he received
his sight and followed him on the way. (Mk 10:46-52)

While I was in Gaza, Israel, I had the opportunity to visit a
school for blind Arab children. It was a heartbreaking experience
as the blind children gathered around me to touch me and to
feel the touch of my hands on them. Through Sister Aloysious,
one of Mother Theresa's Sisters who served as my interpreter,
the children said that they wanted to entertain me. They had
formed a band and wanted me to hear their music.

It was a unique concert. The band leader gave various

directions by tapping on an assortment of wooden blocks emitting different sounds, each sound giving specific directions to the various sections of the band. My heart went out to the blind children of Gaza. I was deeply moved and felt less inhibited since the children could not see me. It was the first concert I ever attended at which my tears flowed freely.

Jesus must have experienced similar deep feelings of compassion when he heard the insistent pleading of Bartimaeus: "Jesus, son of David, have pity on me." His plaintive cry must have touched the heart of Jesus. How eager Jesus was to heal his blindness so that he could enjoy the beauty of creation. Jesus turned away from the "sizable crowd" and said: "Call him." Jesus' question to Bartimaeus seemed rather irrelevant: "What do you want me to do for you?" The answer came immediately and was full of feeling: "Master, I want to see."

The Lord had good reason to ask this question. He wanted to test the man's faith. Since there were only professional beggars in Israel who were required to have some physical handicap, Jesus wanted Bartimaeus to understand that he would have to provide for his own livelihood from now on. He could no longer beg after he had been healed.

Jesus wants to heal all of us so that we can see more clearly with the eyes of faith. He does not impose his healing upon us. He waits until we are open to receive a new vision, a deeper insight into his divine plan for our salvation.

In order to be receptive to his healing, we may have to free ourselves from some attachment, or amend our lives, or make a greater commitment to the Lord. Bartimaeus shows us the way. He threw aside his cloak, jumped up and came to Jesus." At that time a cloak was a very important garment since it served many purposes in daily life. Bartimaeus willingly disposed of his cloak realizing that he would have great difficulty in retrieving it with such a large crowd milling about.

The blind man's spirit of detachment gives us reason to pause and ask ourselves if we are willing to give up our "security blanket" whatever it may be. Is our faith sufficiently strong to permit us to entrust ourselves totally to the Lord regardless of what he may ask of us? Bartimaeus' faith was sufficiently strong to elicit Jesus' comment; "Your faith has saved you." After Bartimaeus received his sight, he followed Jesus up the road. When our vision is broadened, when we can see more clearly the Lord's designs in our life, then we can follow Jesus as he invites us to do.

Even though we may be blessed with 20-20 vision, even though we can see clearly with glasses, we need to pray as Bartimaeus did: "Lord, I want to see." We need greater insight into the infinite, providing, protecting, forgiving, and healing love of God so that we can grow in that love and respond with greater generosity. We need to see our sinfulness, our faults, our weaknesses and then we can pray: "Jesus, son of David, have pity on me." Then, like the blind man, we can follow Jesus on the way.

TWELVE

You Can Make
Me Clean

Now there was a man full of leprosy in one of the towns
where he was; and when he saw Jesus, he fell prostrate,
pleaded with him, and said, "Lord, if you wish, you can
make me clean." Jesus stretched out his hand, touched him,
and said, "I do will it. Be made clean." And the leprosy left
him immediately. Then he ordered him not to tell anyone,
but "Go, show yourself to the priest and offer for your
cleansing what Moses prescribed; that will be proof for
them." The report about him spread all the more, and great
crowds assembled to listen to him and to be cured of their
ailments, but he would withdraw to deserted places to pray.
(Lk 5:12-16)

Dick and Peggy were members of a prayer group for married
couples. They were unable to attend the last meeting, but asked
if they could have a copy of the teaching I usually present at the
meeting. I was happy to oblige.

Soon thereafter on my round of errands one afternoon I
stopped at their home to deliver a copy of the talk I had given.
Shortly after I arrived Paul, a three-year old, rushed in from the
backyard crying out in pain and distress. He had hurt himself

while at play and came running to his mother for comfort and healing. He kept rubbing his eyes with his dirty hands and crying. His besmeared face was quite a sight. Peggy gathered him into her arms and kissed away the tears. His mother's loving embrace and her comforting reassurance quieted the youngster, and a trip to the bathroom washed away the dirt and the tears.

Coincidentally, the talk I had come to deliver to Peggy and Dick was based on the Gospel account of Jesus healing the man covered with leprosy. Just as little Paul ran to his mother in the time of need, so the leper came to Jesus with the heart-rending cry: "Lord, if you wish, you can make me clean." How desperately the leper wanted to be healed. Risking his life he stole away from the leper colony and tried to hide behind any object which would conceal him. He saw his one chance. He dashed up to Jesus realizing that he could be cured or he could be stoned by the crowd.

Jesus understood well the risk which the leper had taken by coming to him begging for a healing. It could mean life or death. Jesus, moved with pity, stretched out his hand, touched him, and said: "I do will it. Be made clean." Jesus could experience the loneliness in the life of this unfortunate man since he was separated from family and friends. Jesus could understand the hopelessness of anyone suffering from such a dreadful and terminal disease that made him or her an outcast of the Jewish community, banned from public places. He could also appreciate the embarrassment and shame which the leper felt because of his hideous appearance. Jesus could see the desperation in the soul of this person whom he loved.

Jesus' heart overflowed with sympathy and compassion. He yearned to bring relief and healing to this man. Reaching out his hand Jesus touched him and immediately the leprosy left him. We can well imagine the great joy which filled the heart of Jesus as the leper rejoiced in his healing. Jesus must have smiled broadly as joy, wonder, and reverence spread throughout the crowd.

In God's sight we are all sinners. Without exception we all at times experience the leprosy of sin. Like the leper, we may have experienced a lack of hope as a passing doubt aroused worry within us, wondering whether the Lord would forgive our repeated infidelities. We might have felt a kind of isolation from others because our sense of guilt overwhelmed us. Perhaps a sense of unworthiness has plagued us over some area of personal difficulty or sin in our lives.

We need to gaze often on this scene, seeing Jesus waiting and longing for the leper to come to him. Down through the ages we can hear the same invitation of Jesus sounding in our own hearts: "Come to me, all you who labor and are burdened, and I will give you rest" (Mt 11:28). What greater burden than the leprosy of sin could we possibly have?

As we approach Jesus we must be willing to acknowledge our faults and failures and place our trust in his healing, forgiving love. With the leper we must say: "Lord, if you will to do so, you can cure me." We can be certain that the heart of Jesus is filled with joy as he says to us: "I do will it. Be made clean."

Say the Word

When he had finished all his words to the people, he entered Capernaum. A centurion there had a slave who was ill and about to die, and he was valuable to him. When he heard about Jesus, he sent elders of the Jews to him, asking him to come and save the life of his slave. They approached Jesus and strongly urged him to come, saying, "He deserves to have you do this for him, for he loves our nation and he built the synagogue for us." And Jesus went with them, but when he was only a short distance from the house, the centurion sent friends to tell him, "Lord, do not trouble yourself, for I am not worthy to have you enter under my roof. Therefore, I did not consider myself worthy to come to you; but say the word and let my servant be healed. For I too am a person subject to authority, with soldiers subject to me. And I say to one, 'Go,' and he goes; and to another, 'Come here,' and he comes; and to my slave, 'Do this,' and he does it." When Jesus heard this he was amazed at him and, turning, said to the crowd following him, "I tell you, not even in Israel have I found such faith." When the messengers returned to the house, they found the slave in good health. (Lk 7:1-10)

In the Gospel we discover that Jesus wanted to keep the centurion front and center in this scene. He is a splendid example for us since he manifested all the essential attitudes we should have when seeking a healing in our own lives or the lives of those who are dear to us.

In the first place, the centurion was a deeply religious man. He had built a synagogue for the Jews to worship their God. He also respected the Jewish law forbidding them to associate with gentiles. For this reason he sent messengers to Jesus instead of coming himself. He did not expect Jesus to come to his home to heal his slave.

This official also showed a loving care and concern for his slave. In those days slaves were considered chattel and could be disposed of at will. Another slave could be obtained for the right sum with little or no difficulty. In fact, the centurion could have obtained another slave with less effort than was required to send a deputation to Jesus begging for a healing for the slave he loved. Surely he was a man of great compassion.

The centurion was also a very humble man. Officers were a proud lot who usually had nothing but hatred and scorn for the Jews. The feeling was mutual since the Jews detested any gentile, especially those who had authority over them. In this case, the centurion rose above all these human considerations. The Jews did the same as they told Jesus: "He deserves to have you do this for him, for he loves our nation and he built the synagogue for us."

The centurion was also a man of great faith. He believed that Jesus had the power to cure his slave. He also trusted that Jesus was gracious enough to perform this healing for him, even though he was a gentile. His faith was so vibrant that he was convinced that Jesus could heal at a distance without laying hands on his slave. Listen to his expression of faith: "Lord, do not trouble yourself, for I am not worthy to have you enter under my roof. Say the word and let my servant be healed."

Jesus was delighted with this profession of faith. His response reveals his pleasure: "I tell you, not even in Israel have I found such faith." Jesus held up the centurion as a paragon of faith. The centurion manifested the attitude of mind and heart with which we should approach the Lord seeking the healing which we need nearly every day of our life. His example is a challenge to us.

In her eucharistic liturgy, the church has immortalized the words of the centurion. As we are about to approach the altar to receive the Lord's healing love in Holy Communion, we pray: Lord, I am not worthy to receive you, but only say the word and I shall be healed." If our faith is as dynamic as that of the centurion, we can be assured that we will be healed. "Only say the word, Lord."

FOURTEEN

Do Not Weep

Soon afterward he journeyed to a city called Nain, and his disciples and a large crowd accompanied him. As he drew near to the gate of the city, a man who had died was being carried out, the only son of his mother, and she was a widow. A large crowd from the city was with her. When the Lord saw her, he was moved with pity for her and said to her, "Do not weep." He stepped forward and touched the coffin; at this the bearers halted, and he said, "Young man, I tell you, arise!" The dead man sat up and began to speak, and Jesus gave him to his mother. Fear seized them all, and they glorified God, exclaiming, "A great prophet has arisen in our midst," and "God has visited his people." This report about him spread through the whole of Judea and in all the surrounding region. (Lk 7:11-17)

During the wake service at my brother's funeral, the Knights of Columbus were praying the rosary. Suddenly in the midst of the rosary, my brother's five-year old granddaughter shouted out: "Haven't we said enough prayers for Grandpa to get well?" At first glance, this outcry might seem quite disruptive and incongruous for such an occasion, but it does demonstrate an understanding of the place and power of prayer in the mind of this five-year old.

Recalling the culture and customs at the time of Jesus, his words to the widowed mother must have seemed equally incongruous to those of his day: "Do not weep." The fact that she was a widow and that this was her only son adds a more somber dimension to this funeral procession. "As he drew near to the gate of the city, a man who had died was being carried out, the only son of his mother, and she was a widow."

Ponder for a moment the full implication of these words. The widowed mother was not simply a mother grieving for her only son, but according to the popular belief of her day, this meant that God was leveling a severe punishment upon her since the family name was dying out. From now on this poor mother would be shunned by the other women of the village. She would not be able to move about the circle of women at the well at eventide. Her presence at the common outdoor bake-oven could be an embarrassment to the villagers.

In spite of this prevalent attitude, or perhaps because of it, Jesus appeared at the gate of the city, stopped the funeral procession and said to the grieving mother: "Do not weep." Let us pause and permit the impact of those words to reach our hearts. Recognize the love and empathy which prompted these words. Listen to the gentleness in his voice as "he was moved with pity for her."

Mark the divine authority over life and death capsulized in the words of Jesus: "Young man, I tell you, arise!" Even though this miraculous healing manifested Jesus' divine power, it was not his primary purpose in restoring this life. Jesus wrought this sign to prove his loving concern for this poor widow. He wants us to know that he is reaching out with that same loving concern to each one of us. We can well visualize the tenderness with which "Jesus gave him to his mother." Words cannot adequately describe this scene. As we contemplate this scene we can experience it only in our hearts.

Jesus' healing presence and his divine power is present with us today and every day of our life in this powerful way. Jesus is present at every deathbed. He is in the midst of the mourners in every funeral home. He is eucharistically present at every Requiem Mass. He may not restore the deceased to physical life, but he is present at the time of death to confer upon the dying person the eternal life of heaven and bring the person into the eternal bliss of heaven with him.

Jesus is present also as a healer at every death. He fills the void of loneliness and emptiness with his peace. His presence softens the sorrow of the bereaved. His love brings strength, comfort, and consolation to all the survivors. His gift of faith is the source of our joy when we realize that a loved one has been taken up into that Trinitarian community of perfect love, which is eternal life with God.

When the crowd in Nain witnessed this miraculous wonder which Jesus performed, they began to praise God in these words: "A great prophet has arisen in our midst," and "God has visited his people." When the moment of our own death arrives, each of us will be alone except for the healing and saving presence of Jesus. He will take us by the hand and lead us into the loving embrace of our heavenly Father.

FIFTEEN

Just Have Faith

When Jesus returned, the crowd welcomed him, for they were all waiting for him. And a man named Jairus, an official of the synagogue, came forward. He fell at the feet of Jesus and begged him to come to his house, because he had an only daughter, about twelve years old, and she was dying. As he went, the crowds almost crushed him.

While he was still speaking, someone from the synagogue official's house arrived and said, "Your daughter is dead; do not trouble the teacher any longer." On hearing this, Jesus answered him, "Do not be afraid; just have faith and she will be saved." When he arrived at the house he allowed no one to enter with him except Peter and John and James, and the child's father and mother. All were weeping and mourning for her, when he said, "Do not weep any longer, for she is not dead, but sleeping." And they ridiculed him, because they knew that she was dead. But he took her by the hand and called to her, "Child, arise!" Her breath returned and she immediately arose. He then directed that she should be given something to eat. Her parents were astounded, and he instructed them to tell no one what had happened. (Lk 8:40-42, 49-56)

Visibly agitated, Joe was telling me how hurt and offended he was the night before when Bill, his best friend, really insulted him and told him their friendship was through. Joe was still angry and upset the next morning when he was telling me about the incident. He told me that he was praying fervently for a total healing and a restoration of their relationship.

I asked Joe if he was genuinely open to receive a healing from the Lord. He assured me that he was. Just at that moment the telephone rang. It was a wrong number and Joe slammed down the phone. He said: "I thought it might be Bill calling to apologize."

"Sorry, Joe," I said, "but you are not open to a healing. You have been waiting for Bill to make the first move. You have placed this condition in your own mind. You will not receive a healing from the Lord until you are able to say 'I forgive.' "

By contrast, in the account of the daughter of Jairus, all the conditions for healing are present. The stage is set perfectly. In the first place, Jairus was the proud president of the synagogue. The members of the synagogue were not friendly to Jesus. In fact, he was barred from teaching in some of them. However, Jairus swallowed his pride and begged Jesus to heal his only daughter. Jesus read the heart of Jairus. He was begging for his daughter's life because he loved her dearly.

One of the first conditions for healing is to ask for it. Jesus said earlier: "Ask and it will be given to you; seek and you will find; knock and the door will be opened to you" (Mt 7:7).

Jesus also wanted the support of his special prayer team. He took Peter, James, and John with him into the girl's house so that they might not only witness the raising of the little girl, but that they might pray for God's will as well. Jesus wanted to teach his chief disciples something about the importance of prayer.

When the disciples were unable to drive the evil spirit out of the little boy, for instance, Jesus assured them: "This kind can only come out through prayer" (Mk 9:29). Jesus was trying to teach his disciples and us how essential prayer is for any healing. Our fervent prayer will dispose us to receive the Lord's healing at so many stages in our life on earth.

Jesus was eager to heal. He did not hesitate in the least to make the journey to the home of the president of the synagogue. He wanted to respond to the faith and trust that Jairus manifested in him by risking criticism of his fellow Jews for going to Jesus with such a request. Jesus always responds to our faith and trust in him.

Jesus was overjoyed to restore the daughter to life and return her to her grieving parents. He recognized their deep love for their only daughter. Perhaps Jesus might have envisioned his own mother's sorrow at the coming death of her only Son on the hill of Calvary.

Jesus also proves his loving sensitivity. While the parents were rejoicing over this tremendous miracle, Jesus reminded them that she was hungry. Jesus did so not only to show his personal concern for the girl, but also to prove that she was really alive and healthy.

Jesus reveals so much about himself by his actions and attitudes in this passage. Every word and every reaction of Jesus gives us a deeper insight into his divine personality. Jesus reveals his boundless love which encourages us to respond in love to him. An awareness of his eagerness to heal us will illumine even our darkest days. Jesus says to us also: "Do not be afraid; just have faith."

SIXTEEN

Who Touched Me?

And a woman afflicted with hemorrhages for twelve years, who [had spent her whole livelihood on doctors and] was unable to be cured by anyone, came up behind him and touched the tassel on his cloak. Immediately her bleeding stopped. Jesus then asked, "Who touched me?" While all were denying it, Peter said, "Master, the crowds are pushing and pressing in upon you." But Jesus said, "Someone has touched me; for I know that power has gone out from me." When the woman realized that she had not escaped notice, she came forward trembling. Falling down before him, she explained in the presence of all the people why she had touched him and how she had been healed immediately. He said to her, "Daughter, your faith has saved you; go in peace." (Lk 8:43-48)

According to an ancient tradition which has neither a scriptural nor an historical basis, Veronica of the sixth station along the way of the cross is the woman whom Jesus cured of the hemorrhage. It was believed that she owned a house in Jerusalem near the spot of the sixth station. If so, she was available to minister to Jesus as he painfully trudged through the streets of Jerusalem on the way of the cross. The tradition is that she wiped away the sweat and blood from the Lord's face when he passed by on his way to Calvary.

When I arrived at the sixth station in the old City of Jerusalem, a large group of pilgrims met head-on with some vendors whose donkeys were loaded with crates of vegetables to be sold in the market. The crowds pressing upon each other reminded me of the crowd surrounding Jesus when the poor woman afflicted with a hemorrhage reached out to touch the tassel of his cloak.

The Gospel describes the scene of the anxious crowd encompassing Jesus. In the midst of that crowd of people was a sick woman who was considered by law to be ceremonially unclean. (Lv 15:19) The Law forbade her to be there since anyone who came in contact with her would also be considered unclean. This poor woman risked the consequences because her great faith assured her that Jesus would heal her if she trusted him.

Be a part of this crowd for a moment. Feel the crowd jostling to get closer to Jesus, to touch him and to hear what he is saying. You may even observe this suffering woman elbowing her way through the crowd to reach Jesus. Let the confusion of this scene fade as we try to get an insight into the mind and heart of Jesus. Try to experience how he felt. He knew the Law, but he also realized the isolation and persecution which this woman endured. She had little or no hope of obtaining a healing from her doctors on whom she "had spent her whole livelihood." Her desperation melted the heart of Jesus.

This account in the Gospel of Luke is just another manifestation of the overwhelming love of the Lord. Imagine the joy which filled the heart of Jesus when he witnessed the great faith of this woman. It was her confidence and trust in the healing power of Jesus which brought her through the throng of people. She risked this venture even though she was ceremonially unclean and would also render anyone who contacted her unclean. The woman's courage and perseverance was augmented by her vibrant faith. Jesus was always pleased when he found people who had faith in him. On the other hand he registered his disappointment when that faith was lacking.

When Jesus asked: "Who touched me?" he did not intend to embarrass her. He wanted to point out how great was her faith and trust in him. He wanted to teach the crowd the importance of faith. Jesus showed his appreciation of her faith by calling her by an endearing title, "Daughter." He also let it be known that it was her strong faith which brought about her healing. "Daughter, your faith has saved you; go in peace."

God permits certain things to happen in our lives so that eventually it will redound to his honor and glory and our growth by helping us have greater faith and trust in him. These happenings may seem rather tragic and traumatic at the time; but when we recall them from the advantage point of the future, we discover what a great blessing they were in our lives.

I am sure that this poor woman's life was drastically changed after the experience of this great healing. She must have become a faithful and dedicated disciple of Jesus. It is also understandable how the tradition began that she was the Veronica along the way of the cross who ministered to Jesus.

SEVENTEEN

Go and Do Likewise

But because he wished to justify himself, he said to Jesus, "And who is my neighbor?" Jesus replied, "A man fell victim to robbers as he went down from Jerusalem to Jericho. They stripped and beat him and went off leaving him half-dead. A priest happened to be going down that road, but when he saw him, he passed by on the opposite side. Likewise a Levite came to the place, and when he saw him, he passed by on the opposite side. But a Samaritan traveler who came upon him was moved with compassion at the sight. He approached the victim, poured oil and wine over his wounds and bandaged them. Then he lifted him up on his own animal, took him to an inn and cared for him. The next day he took out two silver coins and gave them to the innkeeper with the instruction, 'Take care of him. If you spend more than what I have given you, I shall repay you on my way back.' Which of these three, in your opinion, was neighbor to the robbers' victim?" He answered, "The one who treated him with mercy." Jesus said to him, "Go, and do likewise." (Lk 10:29-37)

I was at the airport in Spokane one day to meet a friend arriving on a flight from Minneapolis. The first persons to emerge from the jetway were two stretcher-bearers carrying a passenger who had apparently suffered a serious attack of some kind. Accompanying them was a man who was very solicitous about the stricken person. I learned later that the person who showed such concern about the victim was a medical doctor. I also learned that this was not the doctor's destination, but he had interrupted his flight in order to care for the sick person. Some time later I heard that the doctor's immediate medical attention probably saved the life of the afflicted person. The doctor brought healing to this person very much like the Good Samaritan.

In this unforgettable story in Scripture, we recognize Jesus as the Good Samaritan bringing healing love to the man who fell prey to the robbers. Jesus is a compassionate healer forever bringing healing and relief to everyone who is suffering provided they are receptive to his divine gift of healing.

In discussing love of neighbor with the lawyer who posed the problem, Jesus explained that the love of God and the love of neighbor superseded all other considerations. In this parable the priest and the Levite who passed by were probably on their way to participate in the temple worship. According to the customs and the many and various interpretations of the rabbinical law, they would have been barred from worshiping in the temple because having gone near what appeared to be a corpse they would have become unclean. They would have had to have waited for many days to be purified.

The point which Jesus was trying to make is that the love of God and neighbor takes precedence over all other customs and laws when someone is in dire need. Jesus is infinitely compassionate. He is eager to heal us when we are hurting spiritually, psychologically, or physically. Jesus fulfills the role of the Good Samaritan any time we stand in need of his healing power. And that happens every day, not only in dire circumstances.

When we are hurt because of misunderstanding, criticism, or persecution, Jesus is present with his healing love to soothe our pain by filling our hearts to overflowing with his love. Thus he frees us of any anger, rancor, or bitterness which might well up within us. His healing love enables us to say "I forgive." Only God's love can bring us to this stage of growth.

In our day physical violence is not uncommon. Be assured that Jesus is there as the Good Samaritan to come to our aid, just as he inspired and motivated the compassionate doctor on that flight from Minneapolis to care for someone who was seriously ill. Jesus is also the divine Physician soothing our pain and agony in times of illness by sharing his peace and joy with us. He enlightens the medical staff who come to our aid as well.

In this parable, Jesus is encouraging us to be compassionate toward others, especially those in need. He entreats us to let his compassion radiate through us. Compassion is not only a profound feeling for the misfortune of others, but it is also a willingness and a desire to come to the aid of some afflicted person, even if it causes us some inconvenience and sacrifice.

Jesus urges us to be compassionate: "Be merciful, just as [also] your Father is merciful" (Lk 6:36). When we have experienced the healing compassion of Jesus, then we will more readily want to reach out in loving compassion toward anyone whom the Lord sends to us. Let us be ready and willing to serve them, even if it is inconvenient.

EIGHTEEN

She Stood Up Straight

He was teaching in a synagogue on the sabbath. And a woman was there who for eighteen years had been crippled by a spirit; she was bent over, completely incapable of standing erect. When Jesus saw her, he called to her and said, "Woman, you are set free of your infirmity." He laid his hands on her, and she at once stood up straight and glorified God. But the leader of the synagogue, indignant that Jesus had cured on the sabbath, said to the crowd in reply, "There are six days when work should be done. Come on those days to be cured, not on the sabbath day." The Lord said to him in reply, "Hypocrites! Does not each one of you on the sabbath untie his ox or his ass from the manger and lead it out for watering? This daughter of Abraham, whom Satan has bound for eighteen years now, ought she not to have been set free on the sabbath day from this bondage?" When he said this, all his adversaries were humiliated; and the whole crowd rejoiced at all the splendid deeds done by him. (Lk 13:10-17)

For eighteen long years the poor crippled woman in the Gospel suffered from her malady. "She was bent over, completely incapable of standing erect." For all those years she could only look at people's feet without seeing their faces. She could see only the lower trunk of a tree and could not behold the beauty of the whole tree. She could not enjoy the sight of a moonlit night nor admire the starry skies overhead. With this terrible affliction her world was barely above ground or floor level.

How fortunate she was to come to the synagogue on that sabbath when Jesus was teaching. When Jesus saw her bearing this affliction without complaining, his heart immediately went out to her. How tenderly he must have touched her. What healing power there was in that divine touch. Luke says: "He laid his hands on her, and she at once stood up straight and glorified God."

This is just another example of Jesus' healing love reaching out to those who were in distress and who were willing to be healed. In his glory Jesus continues his healing mission among us. How fortunate we are!

It is possible that we are suffering from a similar malady. It may be a psychological rather than a physical deformity. We may have a rather negative attitude which causes us to look downward and miss the beauty of God's creation, especially in our fellow human beings. We may see only in passing and fail to appreciate the exquisite beauty of a gorgeous sunset. A negative attitude robs us of our peace. We may fail to appreciate the gleeful laughter of a baby experiencing the newness and freshness of life. We miss so many beautiful things in life when we adopt this kind of attitude.

If we are plagued with an attitude of fear, worry, or anxiety, we will never be able to appreciate the fine virtues and qualities of another person. Looking continually at a person's feet instead of into their eyes, for example, may create a critical and judgmental attitude toward them. If we are always focusing on another's faults, we will be betraying our own. Such an attitude will never permit us to be a happy person and enjoy life to the full.

If our attitude of the heart and mind is bent over, it will be difficult, if not impossible, to permit our smile to radiate to others who need our affirmation and encouragement at critical times in their lives. If we recognize any of these traits in ourselves, we stand in need of a healing. Jesus is our healer, always ready and eager to lay his healing hand upon us, just as he did for the poor crippled woman. He wants to focus our attention on the horizons of life that our joy may be full.

When Jesus healed this crippled woman on the sabbath, he was severely criticized by the leader of the synagogue. Jesus called their bluff. He quoted their own interpretation of the law at them. "Hypocrites! Does not each one of you on the sabbath untie his ox or his ass from the manger and lead it out for watering?" Jesus was impatient with their private interpretations of the law when the law of charity demanded immediate action. He pointed out how the rights of the individual and the demands of love supersede all human interpretations of the law by quoting this example.

In fact, Jesus gave them an even greater reason by pointing to this particular healing on the sabbath. Eighteen years was a long, long time for this poor woman to be suffering from such an infirmity. His love for her could not wait. He reached out immediately and without hesitation to heal her.

Jesus lives on in our lives today. He is always eager and anxious to heal us. He only asks that we be willing to accept his healing love.

NINETEEN

Is It Lawful?

On a sabbath he went to dine at the home of one of the leading Pharisees, and the people there were observing him carefully. In front of him there was a man suffering from dropsy. Jesus spoke to the scholars of the law and Pharisees in reply, asking, "Is it lawful to cure on the sabbath or not?" But they kept silent; so he took the man and, after he had healed him, dismissed him. Then he said to them, "Who among you, if your son or ox falls into a cistern, would not immediately pull him out on the sabbath day?" But they were unable to answer his question. (Lk 14:1-6)

Jim and Helen had a happy marriage. Throughout the years their mutual love grew and matured with each passing year. Both of them knew suffering but in a different way. Helen had dropsy. Jim suffered along with her at each stage of her illness.

As the excess fluid filled her system, Jim lovingly cared for her and nursed her tenderly. His compassionate heart ached for her. The empathy he felt was written in every line of his face. He prayed continually and fervently for a complete healing for Helen.

If we could add a divine dimension to Jim's great compassion for his wife, we could better fathom the overwhelming compassion which Jesus had for the man who was suffering from dropsy. When Jesus observed the man's body bloated with excess fluid, he immediately healed him heedless of the sabbath regulations. Jesus understood how much this man was suffering. His divine love demanded immediate action. The calendar could not delay the cure. Jesus was also aware that he was under intense scrutiny. "The people there were observing him carefully."

Without hesitation Jesus cured the man and sent him on his way. Jesus knew what the Pharisees were thinking. Jesus defended his action by quoting their own interpretation of the law to them. "Who among you, if your son or ox falls into a cistern, would not immediately pull him out on the sabbath day?" His loving concern for the afflicted should have endeared Jesus to everyone. His compassion knew no limits as he reached out to anyone who needed healing.

On the contrary it did just the opposite for his enemies. Jesus was not defying or violating the lawful sabbath observance. He was merely demonstrating the injustices of certain overly legalistic interpretations and regulations of the law. Did he succeed in breaking through their hardness of heart? No, but he continued to take every opportunity to teach them how the dictates of the law of love must take precedence over all other laws. He made the love of God and love of neighbor the first and foremost law.

The many healings which Jesus performed can have a transforming power in our own lives today. In the first place, Jesus demonstrated the serenity with which he approached life. There is nothing more trying than to be under constant and critical scrutiny. Such scrutiny can cause a person to lose his nerve as well as his temper and cause a person to become constantly irritable. As we contemplate Jesus' reactions under these trying conditions, we will find help when we are thrust into similar irritating situations. We will grow from observing his example.

Second, Jesus always accepted an invitation of hospitality. Jesus was showing us by his example that if we wish to make our enemies our friends, we must meet them and talk with them. Such communication can be the beginning of a healing process.

Third, by his words and actions, Jesus is teaching us that the law of love far exceeds many of the trifling regulations which arise in life. We can permit these relatively unimportant happenings to fill our whole horizon and disturb our sense of peace. A proper perspective is not only a powerful preventative against the wrong kind of attitude, but also a source of great healing for our own lives.

As we contemplate prayerfully the healing of the man suffering from dropsy, we will come to a better appreciation of the compassion of Jesus and his loving concern for anyone who is afflicted in any way. This prayer posture will give us insights into the personality of Jesus far beyond mere observation and analysis. Furthermore, since we become what we contemplate or dwell on, we too will experience greater compassion in our relationships with others. This is what Jesus meant when he advised us: "Learn from me, for I am meek and humble of heart; and you will find rest for yourselves" (Mt 11:29).

TWENTY

Places of Honor

He told a parable to those who had been invited, noticing how they were choosing the places of honor at the table. "When you are invited by someone to a wedding banquet, do not recline at table in the place of honor. A more distinguished guest than you may have been invited by him, and the host who invited both of you may approach you and say, 'Give your place to this man,' and then you would proceed with embarrassment to take the lowest place. Rather, when you are invited, go and take the lowest place so that when the host comes to you he may say, 'My friend, move up to a higher position.' Then you will enjoy the esteem of your companions at the table. For everyone who exalts himself will be humbled, but the one who humbles himself will be exalted." (Lk 14:7-11)

I attended one of the many art shows at which Laura's works of art were exhibited. She is a gifted and talented artist who works in various media. She is also a prayerful person with a close relationship to the Lord. When someone recognized her work and congratulated and commended her for her accomplishments, she would respond with a little smile and low-keyed "Thank-you." Then I noticed that she would often close her eyes for a moment. Eventually, I learned that she had formed the habit of saying a quiet prayer to herself after she received compliments: "Thank you, Lord, may it bring you glory." This is the kind of humility which Jesus was trying to impress upon his hearers when he suggested that they take the lowest places at a wedding party.

In his day the seating arrangement at gatherings was always a source of contention. The Pharisees always claimed the places of honor. Today many have partially solved that problem by using place cards to arrange seating at special banquets for events like weddings.

Jesus used this confrontation as an opportunity to teach and to show us the way to true healing in his kingdom. Jesus put ordinary experiences of life into the framework of a parable to guide us into his way of life. Jesus not only warned us against our pride, he also pointed to imitation of his own lifestyle as a means to healing our pride.

Is there anyone among us who does not need healing from the pride which creeps into our life so easily? Our pride surfaces under many different guises—wounded feelings, lack of recognition, criticism, rejection, and in so many other ways. When we show our Achilles heel, the tempter has a field day. How much we need the Lord's healing in this area!

Humility stands in direct opposition to pride. Humility is the truth—the truth about ourselves and the truth about God. What have we that he has not given us? Truly God has gifted us. And when we acknowledge and use our gifts as the Lord intends, then we are truly humble. On the other hand pride urges us to take all the credit ourselves.

There are subtle ways in which our pride sallies forth. Pride prompts us to use as an excuse a lack of time or limited giftedness for not doing a better job, rather than to admit honestly our own limitations. This is often called humility with a hook because in reality we are trying to snare another compliment. In the parable of taking the lowest place and on many other occasions, Jesus instructed us in the way of humility. It is the opposite of pride. Genuine humility will heal us of our pride.

Second, Jesus' whole life is one prolonged act of humility, from his birth in a cave through the hostile rejection and persecution he suffered at the hands of his enemies. Jesus rose above all these attacks because of his humility. He begged us to learn from his example. "Learn from me, for I am meek and humble of heart" (Mt 11:29).

Third, Jesus set the example for us as Christians to follow. After washing the feet of the apostles in the Upper Room, he challenged us:

> "Do you realize what I have done for you? You call me 'teacher' and 'master,' and rightly so, for indeed I am. If I, therefore, the master and teacher, have washed your feet, you ought to wash one another's feet. I have given you a model to follow, so that as I have done for you, you should also do." (Jn 13:12-15)

Jesus' humility reached a superb climax when he laid down his life for us. "He humbled himself, becoming obedient to death, even death on a cross" (Phil 2:8).

Most of us will struggle to overcome and conquer our pride all the days of our life. Jesus was well aware of the battle we would face. He remains with us to continue to heal us of our pride by his instruction on humility, his example, and his healing love.

TWENTY ONE

He Ran to His Son

Then he said, "A man had two sons, and the younger son said to his father, 'Father, give me the share of your estate that should come to me.' So the father divided the property between them. After a few days, the younger son collected all his belongings and set off to a distant country where he squandered his inheritance on a life of dissipation. When he had freely spent everything, a severe famine struck that country, and he found himself in dire need. So he hired himself out to one of the local citizens who sent him to his farm to tend the swine. And he longed to eat his fill of the pods on which the swine fed, but nobody gave him any. Coming to his senses he thought, 'How many of my father's hired workers have more than enough food to eat, but here am I, dying from hunger. I shall get up and go to my father and I shall say to him, "Father, I have sinned against heaven and against you. I no longer deserve to be called your son; treat me as you would treat one of your hired workers."' So he got up and went back to his father. While he was still a long way off, his father caught sight of him, and was filled with compassion. He ran to his son, embraced him and kissed him. His son said to him 'Father, I have sinned against heaven and against you; I no longer deserve to be called your son.' But his father ordered his servants, 'Quickly bring the finest robe and put it on him; put a ring on his finger and sandals on his feet. Take the fattened calf and slaughter it. Then let us celebrate with a feast, because this son of mine was dead, and has come to life again; he was lost, and has been found.' Then the celebration began. Now the older son had been out in the field and, on his way back, as he neared the house, he heard the sound of music and dancing. He called one of the servants and asked what this might mean. The servant said to him, 'Your brother has returned and your father has slaughtered the fattened calf because he has him back safe and sound.' He became angry, and when he refused to enter the house, his father came out and pleaded with him. He said to his father in reply, 'Look, all these years I served you and not once did I disobey your orders; yet you never gave me even a young goat to feast on with my friends. But when your son returns who swallowed up your property with prostitutes, for him you slaughter the fattened calf.' He said to him, 'My son, you are here with me always; everything I have is yours. But now we must celebrate and rejoice, because your brother was dead and has come to life again; he was lost and has been found.' " (Lk 15:11-32)

Bob peered through the early morning darkness across the street from his home. It was still too dark to read the sign posted on the front of the door. Dare he approach any closer?

Some weeks before in a fit of rebellion, he had stormed out of the house vowing never to return. In a very short time he discovered that the world did not need or even want a penniless youth. Maybe his family did not want him either after this escapade, he thought to himself. With his pulse beating faster and with hesitant steps, he started to cross the street to read the poster on the front door of his home. What a surprise for him to read clearly the message: "Welcome home, Bob, we miss you and we love you!"

At that precise moment his father dashed out the front door and down the steps to welcome him home. Their animated conversation in the living room awakened the whole family as everyone tumbled out of bed and came in to welcome back their wayward son and brother.

In our weakness and brokenness we may have strayed away from the family of God into which we have been adopted. In this parable Jesus gives us a picture of how temptation can lead us away from our spiritual family. More important, he gives us the reassurance that the mercy and compassion, the enduring and healing love of the Father is always ready and eager to welcome us home.

In Psalm 1, the writer cautions us about how we can gradually withdraw from the Lord and the family of God. Notice the line of development. First, the wayward one follows the counsel of the wicked; then he walks in the way of sinners; and finally he sits in their company.

In the younger brother we see all the elements of drifting into sin. However, as he began to experience the cruel indifference of the world, a conversion process began to take place in his heart. Fortunately the younger son had the humility and the courage to acknowledge his waywardness and to seek reconciliation.

However, in this parable Jesus intends our focus to be fixed on the father. The father in this story is obviously our loving Father in heaven, and we are personified in the younger son. In this story the father was ever alert and looking for the return of his son. The vigilance of the father is described in these words: "While he was still a long way off, his father caught sight of him, and was filled with compassion. He ran to his son, embraced him and kissed him."

Our heavenly Father waits patiently for us. When we recognize and acknowledge our waywardness, and when we seek reconciliation, our compassionate Father runs to meet us. Someone has said that if we take one step toward our Father, he will take the remaining ninety-nine steps to meet us.

The sinful son in this parable wanted to confess his guilt and beg for forgiveness. He wanted to be considered only as a hired servant. The father would have none of it. He not only forgave him long before he could ask for forgiveness, but he reinstated him in the family with all the rights and privileges of a son. The robe which the father ordered signifies restoration with full honors to the family. The ring is symbolic of full authority. Only children of the family wore shoes, the slaves and servants did not. This meant that the past was gone, forgiven and forgotten.

In this parable of the lost son, Jesus intended to teach us various lessons. The principal point he was trying to make was that the Father is more anxious to forgive and heal us than we may be to receive his forgiveness and healing. We need only approach him with the appropriate attitude of mind and heart. "A heart contrite and humbled, O God, you will not spurn" (Ps 51:19).

TWENTY TWO

Where Are the Other Nine?

As he continued his journey to Jerusalem, he traveled
through Samaria and Galilee. As he was entering a village,
ten lepers met [him]. They stood at a distance from him and
raised their voice, saying, "Jesus, Master! Have pity on us!"
And when he saw them, he said, "Go show yourselves to the
priests." As they were going they were cleansed. And one of
them, realizing he had been healed, returned, glorifying
God in a loud voice; and he fell at the feet of Jesus and
thanked him. He was a Samaritan. Jesus said in reply, "Ten
were cleansed, were they not? Where are the other nine? Has
none but this foreigner returned to give thanks to God?"
Then he said to him, "Stand up and go; your faith has saved
you." (Lk 17:11-19)

Some years ago I was asked to celebrate the Eucharist on
Thanksgiving Day for a group of children who were accompanied by their parents. Before beginning the Mass, we placed
a blackboard in the front part of the church. We began the
ceremony by asking any child under twelve years to mention a
special gift or blessing for which they wished to thank God on
this Thanksgiving Day. As they mentioned the gift for which

they were most grateful, we wrote it down on the blackboard.

I was happily surprised to see how many times the children mentioned that they were thankful to God for their parents or for something which their parents had done for them. Needless to say, their parents were beaming with satisfaction. It was obvious that the parents really appreciated being thanked publicly by their children.

Jesus used the episode of the healing of the ten lepers to teach us two valuable lessons: the power of his healing love and the importance of gratitude. One day as Jesus journeyed along ten lepers stood at a distance and cried out to him: "Jesus, Master! Have pity on us!" These men had been afflicted with this dreadful disease—the AIDS of the biblical era. The victims of leprosy were social outcasts, misfits, and rejects. They won the heart of Jesus. Jesus advised them to show themselves to the priests who had the authority to admit them back into the community if they were sufficiently healed. This was a test of their faith for it was only "as they were going they were cleansed."

Of the ten who were cleansed only one returned to express his gratitude. "And one of them, realizing he had been healed, returned, glorifying God in a loud voice; and he fell at the feet of Jesus and thanked him."

Jesus was obviously disappointed. He said: "Ten were cleansed, were they not? Where are the other nine?" Were not the other nine grateful for their miraculous healing? For this sign of God's healing love? Jesus was pleased to heal these lepers from this loathsome disease. He likewise longs to heal us from anything which is preventing us from deepening our relationship with him, especially the leprosy of sin.

Jesus assures us that he will heal us if we really trust him and if we are disposed to receive his healing love. Notice that he first sent the ten lepers on their way to be examined by the priests. The lepers trusted Jesus and set out immediately to see the priests. "As they were going, they were cleansed." If they had doubted either his power to heal or his desire to heal them, they might have hesitated or even refused to be on their way.

Jesus asks the same trust from us. At times we may feel that Jesus does not really want to heal us, or that we are not worthy to ask or receive such a blessing from him. Only faith and trust can change this attitude.

The second great lesson which Jesus teaches is gratitude. Jesus registered his deep disappointment when only one of the ten returned to praise and thank God. That is a very low percentage. We need to ask ourselves if our own percentage is even as high as one out of ten. We can best manifest our appreciation for a gift by an expression of gratefulness and then by using the gift for the purpose for which God intends it.

When Jesus heals us of some fault or failing, of some worry or anxiety, of some fear or resentment, we can show our appreciation by verbalizing our thanks and also by stepping out in a greater loving and committed service to others. When we stand in need of any kind of healing, may our prayer be the humble plea of the lepers: "Jesus, Master! Have pity on us!" Should Jesus ask: "Where are the other nine?" we can rejoice and say: "Here we are, Lord, praising and thanking you."

TWENTY THREE

Come Down Quickly

He came to Jericho and intended to pass through the town. Now a man there named Zacchaeus, who was a chief tax collector and also a wealthy man, was seeking to see who Jesus was; but he could not see him because of the crowd, for he was short in stature. So he ran ahead and climbed a sycamore tree in order to see Jesus, who was about to pass that way. When he reached the place, Jesus looked up and said to him, "Zacchaeus, come down quickly, for today I must stay at your house." And he came down quickly and received him with joy. When they all saw this, they began to grumble, saying, "He has gone to stay at the house of a sinner." But Zacchaeus stood there and said to the Lord, "Behold, half of my possessions, Lord, I shall give to the poor, and if I have extorted anything from anyone I shall repay it four times over." And Jesus said to him, "Today salvation has come to this house because this man too is a descendant of Abraham. For the Son of Man has come to seek and to save what was lost." (Lk 19:1-10)

It all happened on a school bus transporting high school students to and from their homes. Donna was not the most popular girl in the school even though she did have a gracious personality. Her excessive weight and general appearance would not pose any serious competition in a beauty contest.

On the bus, Donna was often the target of jibes, ridicule, and even insults. She usually sat alone.

One day when the attack on Donna seemed especially vicious Steve, a hefty sophomore, went back and sat beside her. Without a word he simply glared at each one of the students who had been taunting Donna. An ominous silence settled on all in the bus. Even the driver turned his head to see what had happened. Steve dared to be different and that took courage. His reaction to the relentless teasing directed toward Donna was certainly Christlike.

In Jericho, Jesus reacted in a similar fashion when Zacchaeus was unjustly persecuted by his own people. As a tax collector, Zacchaeus was the object of scorn and derision. He was hated and despised. He felt lonely and rejected. His job of collecting taxes made him an outcast. Zacchaeus had heard that Jesus was friendly to tax collectors and sinners. He wanted to get at least a glimpse of Jesus, but the crowd would not give him a place in the forefront.

Zacchaeus risked making a fool of himself by climbing into a sycamore tree in order to see Jesus as he passed by. In doing so he left himself open to even more ridicule. But that did not deter Zacchaeus, for a kind of faith was stirring in his heart.

When Jesus arrived on the scene, he reached out in loving concern to Zacchaeus. "When he reached the place, Jesus looked up and said to him, 'Zacchaeus, come down quickly, for today I must stay at your house.' " Jesus accepted Zacchaeus just as he was.

The crowd was startled at the words of Jesus. They were amazed that Jesus would not only recognize this despised tax collector, but that he would actually be willing to become a guest in his home. That kind of hospitality was positively forbidden in those days for law-abiding Jews. No doubt Zacchaeus was also surprised beyond words.

Jesus' acceptance of Zacchaeus initiated a tremendous healing process and conversion in him. Zacchaeus was properly disposed to receive the Lord's forgiveness and healing. He was a humble man as his efforts to see Jesus indicated. He was also a man of great faith, otherwise he would have had some misgivings about Jesus' attitude toward him.

Tax collectors had the reputation of being extremely unjust in exacting more than the required amount of taxes in order to feather their own nests. This is why some men accepted this job. When no one volunteered for this position, Rome simply appointed a person to collect the taxes for them. We do not know whether or not Zacchaeus was unwillingly appointed by the Romans.

Zacchaeus proved his good will and receptivity to Jesus' acceptance of him. A conversion process was taking place within him. Gradually that conversion was complete. He happily announced: "Behold, half of my possessions, Lord, I shall give to the poor, and if I have extorted anything from anyone I shall repay it four times over."

Lord Jesus, your loving acceptance of Zacchaeus wrought a complete conversion in him and brought him salvation. In your compassionate love, you accept us regardless of who we are or what we have done. Help us to accept all those you send across our path with that same loving concern you have for us. Then together we can enjoy that lasting peace and friendship which only you can give.

TWENTY FOUR

Stay with Us

Now that very day two of them were going to a village seven miles from Jerusalem called Emmaus, and they were conversing about all the things that had occurred. And it happened that while they were conversing and debating, Jesus himself drew near and walked with them, but their eyes were prevented from recognizing him. He asked them, "What are you discussing as you walk along?" They stopped, looking downcast. One of them, named Cleopas, said to him in reply, "Are you the only visitor to Jerusalem who does not know of the things that have taken place there in these days?" And he replied to them, "What sort of things?" They said to him, "The things that happened to Jesus the Nazarene, who was a prophet mighty in deed and word before God and all the people, how our chief priests and rulers both handed him over to a sentence of death and crucified him. But we were hoping that he would be the one to redeem Israel; and besides all this, it is now the third day since this took place. Some women from our group, however, have astounded us: they were at the tomb early in the morning and did not find his body; they came back and reported that they had indeed seen a vision of angels who announced that he was alive. Then some of those with us went to the tomb and found things just as the women had described, but him they did not see." And he said to them, "Oh, how foolish you are! How slow of heart to believe all that the prophets spoke! Was it not necessary that the Messiah should suffer these things and enter his glory?" Then beginning with Moses and all the prophets, he interpreted to them what referred to him in all the scriptures. As they approached the village to which they were going, he gave the impression that he was going on farther. But they urged him, "Stay with us, for it is nearly evening and the day is almost over." So he went in to stay with them. And it happened that, while he was with them at table, he took bread, said the blessing, broke it, and gave it to them. With that their eyes were opened and they recognized him, but he vanished from their sight. Then they said to each other, "Were not our hearts burning [within us] while he spoke to us on the way and opened the scriptures to us?" So they set out at once and returned to Jerusalem where they found gathered together the eleven and those with them who were saying, "The Lord has truly been raised and has appeared to Simon!" Then the two recounted what had taken place on the way and how he was made known to them in the breaking of the bread. (Lk 24:13-35)

Walking on the grounds of a retreat house one day, I discovered a rather long, rugged pathway which seemed to hug the perimeter of the extensive piece of property. I noticed that the area had been left in its natural beauty with no formal plantings along the pathway. There are several hills and valleys to be negotiated as one walks along the way. To my amazement this pathway had been named the Road to Emmaus.

This is an ideal choice of names since the same kind of experience the disciples had along the road to Emmaus can happen along this route as retreatants take meditative walks to seek the Lord. Just so in the Gospel account of the Emmaus journey, the two disciples were making their way, clearly downcast and discouraged. Their hopes and dreams of a liberating Messiah had been shattered when Jesus was executed as a common criminal. The disciples needed time to meditate and reflect along the way.

Yet even as they made their way toward Emmaus with heavy hearts, "Jesus himself drew near and walked with them, but their eyes were prevented from recognizing him." Jesus came to them as a healer. He wanted to lift the burden of despondency and discouragement which weighed heavily upon them. He captured their attention by chiding them: "Oh, how foolish you are! How slow of heart to believe all that the prophets spoke!" When Jesus aroused their curiosity and they were prepared to listen to him, he began by opening the Scriptures to them. His Word was gradually becoming a healing word.

Jesus brought healing to their hearts through three avenues. His very presence brought healing to these discouraged disciples. He listened to them and let them tell him about everything that had taken place in Jerusalem over the past few days. His listening manifested his loving concern for them. The healing was beginning to take effect in them. Second, he explained the Scriptures in such a way that they could say later: "Were not our hearts burning [within us] while he spoke to us on the way and opened the scriptures to us?" Third, the Mass which Jesus celebrated with them ministered healing. The Mass is a Sacrament of healing. Through the Mass Jesus continues his healing mission among us.

Each day we make our own journey to Emmaus. This is what the walk at the retreat house signified to me. Our trek to our own village of Emmaus may be our regular journey to our place of employment or business. It may be a shopping trip, a visit to a friend, or it may take place in our own home as we perform our household duties.

As we journey along we may be like the disciples, preoccupied with all our personal interests or burdened with numerous duties and responsibilities. Even though Jesus promised to be with us and within us at every moment of the day, we are not always consciously aware of his journeying along with us. We, too, like the disciples can become weary and discouraged. Bringing ourselves to an awareness of his abiding presence and love can produce a powerful healing in us.

Jesus is present in a special way in his Word. His Word brings us hope and encouragement, inspiration and motivation, comfort and consolation. It empowers us to fulfill the daily demands made upon us. His Word has the power to heal.

At Mass Jesus is eucharistically present. Jesus shares his divine life and love with us. He will heal our disappointments and discouragement, our hurts and pain, our fatigue and exhaustion. Jesus comes to us as a healer at Mass and in the everyday experiences of life. Jesus is pleased when we come to him seeking and imploring his healing. To receive the out-pouring of his healing love, we, like the disciples, must beg him to "stay with us, for it is nearly evening and the day is almost over." Come, Lord Jesus, come!

TWENTY FIVE

What Good Are These for So Many?

After this, Jesus went across the Sea of Galilee [of Tiberias].
A large crowd followed him, because they saw the signs he
was performing on the sick. Jesus went up on the mountain,
and there he sat down with his disciples. The Jewish feast of
Passover was near. When Jesus raised his eyes and saw that a
large crowd was coming to him, he said to Philip, "Where
can we buy enough food for them to eat?" He said this to test
him, because he himself knew what he was going to do.
Philip answered him, "Two hundred days' wages worth of
food would not be enough for each of them to have a little
[bit]." One of his disciples, Andrew, the brother of Simon
Peter, said to him, "There is a boy here who has five barley
loaves and two fish; but what good are these for so many?"
Jesus said, "Have the people recline." Now there was a great
deal of grass in that place. So the men reclined, about five
thousand in number. Then Jesus took the loaves, gave
thanks, and distributed them to those who were reclining,
and also as much of the fish as they wanted. When they had
had their fill, he said to his disciples, "Gather the fragments
left over, so that nothing will be wasted." So they collected
them, and filled twelve wicker baskets with fragments from

the five barley loaves that had been more than they could eat. When the people saw the sign he had done, they said, "This is truly the Prophet, the one who is to come into the world." Since Jesus knew that they were going to come and carry him off to make him king, he withdrew again to the mountain alone. (Jn 6:1-15)

When a Christian community in El Paso, Texas, reflected on the words of Jesus: "I was hungry and you gave me food," they decided it was time to respond to the Lord's admonition. They agreed to prepare a Christmas dinner for the poor people who lived the life of scavengers at the dump across the border in Juarez, Mexico. These poor people eked out a miserable existence by scavenging bits and morsels of food which had been thrown into the garbage dump. They also searched for articles which could be recycled for which they received a mere pittance.

On this memorable Christmas Day, even though this community of Christians from El Paso had not prepared a sufficient amount of food for the vast multitude of people living there, the supply of food was never exhausted. It seemed to replenish itself as they continued to distribute it. This manifestation of the Lord's divine power and loving concern recalls the miraculous healings of Jesus during his earthly ministry.

On one occasion when Jesus saw the large crowd gathering around him, he sensed the dual hunger within them. They were hungry in body and in spirit. They had followed Jesus without any food and their physical hunger kept gnawing at them. They were also spiritually hungry for the Word of eternal life. Jesus was eager to satisfy both with his healing power.

Jesus knew that they were weakened from a lack of food and that they were far from home. They were also so eager to hear the Word of God that they risked going without food. Think for a moment about the concern and love of Jesus as he gazed out over that multitude surrounding him. He wanted to satisfy their hunger, but he also wanted to test the faith of the apostles and all the people. That test came when he asked Philip, "Where can we buy enough food for them to eat?" John tells us in his Gospel that Jesus was testing Philip's faith, for he "knew what he was going to do."

Philip gave the Lord the kind of practical answer that most of us can readily relate to. "Two hundred days' wages worth of food would not be enough for each of them to have a little." He laid out the facts of the matter.

But the apostle Andrew stepped out in faith—even if his faith was a mere mustard seed—and paved the way for the Lord to act. He said to Jesus, "There is a boy here who has five barley loaves and two fish; but what good are these for so many"? With that, Jesus told the apostles to have the people sit down and then miraculously multiplied the loaves and fish.

The miracle of the loaves and fish greatly increased the faith of the apostles and all the people. They witnessed a clear demonstration of his power. In fact, the people began to acclaim him as "the Prophet, the one who is to come into the world."

Jesus' purpose extended, however, far beyond meeting their physical needs or their expectations for a political messiah who would save them from the tyranny of Rome. He wanted to satisfy their spiritual hunger. The people of his day were eagerly awaiting *the Messiah*. These people were not only curious about the mission of Jesus, their faith in him had also begun to take root and blossom. They were hungry and thirsty for the good news he came to proclaim. After they witnessed the miracle of the multiplication of the loaves and fishes, they were better prepared to accept Jesus' next teaching. He had come to satisfy their spiritual hunger also. This is accomplished by giving them and us the eucharistic gift of himself. Later in this same chapter, John records the promise which Jesus made in these words: "I am the bread of life; whoever comes to me will never hunger, and whoever believes in me will never thirst" (Jn 6:35).

As the Bread of Life, Jesus came to satisfy the spiritual hunger in all of us. We all hunger for a more personal and a more intimate union with him. Jesus gave us the Eucharist as the sacramental channel of healing in our everyday Christian life. In the Eucharist, Jesus heals by his divine presence and also through his Word. It is Jesus' wish that we "do this in memory of me," so that he can continue to extend his healing presence and power among us.

Let us approach the table of the Lord with expectant faith, even if it is a mere mustard seed. The Lord will multiply it and come to us in the Eucharist with his healing presence and saving power.

TWENTY SIX

He Went and Washed

As he passed by he saw a man blind from birth. His disciples asked him, "Rabbi, who sinned, this man or his parents, that he was born blind?" Jesus answered, "Neither he nor his parents sinned; it is so that the works of God might be made visible through him. We have to do the works of the one who sent me while it is day. Night is coming when no one can work. While I am in the world, I am the light of the world." When he had said this, he spat on the ground and made clay with the saliva, and smeared the clay on his eyes, and said to him, "Go wash in the Pool of Siloam" (which means Sent). So he went and washed, and came back able to see.

His neighbors and those who had seen him earlier as a beggar said, "Isn't this the one who used to sit and beg?" Some said, "It is," but others said, "No, he just looks like him." He said, "I am." So they said to him, "[So] how were your eyes opened?" He replied, "The man called Jesus made clay and anointed my eyes and told me, 'Go to Siloam and wash.' So I went there and washed and was able to see." And they said to him, "Where is he?" He said, "I don't know."

They brought the one who was once blind to the Pharisees. Now Jesus had made clay and opened his eyes on a sabbath. So then the Pharisees also asked him how he was able to see. He said to them, "He put clay on my eyes, and I washed, and now I can see." So some of the Pharisees said,

"This man is not from God, because he does not keep the sabbath." [But] others said, "How can a sinful man do such signs?" And there was a division among them. So they said to the blind man again, "What do you have to say about him, since he opened your eyes?" He said, "He is a prophet."

. . . a second time they called the man who had been blind and said to him, "Give God the praise! We know that this man is a sinner." He replied, "If he is a sinner, I do not know. One thing I do know is that I was blind and now I see." So they said to him, "What did he do to you? How did he open your eyes?" He answered them, "I told you already and you did not listen. Why do you want to hear it again? Do you want to become his disciples, too?" They ridiculed him and said, "You are that man's disciple; we are disciples of Moses! We know that God spoke to Moses, but we do not know where this one is from." The man answered and said to them, "This is what is so amazing, that you do not know where he is from, yet he opened my eyes. We know that God does not listen to sinners, but if one is devout and does his will, he listens to him. It is unheard of that anyone ever opened the eyes of a person born blind. If this man were not from God, he would not be able to do anything." They answered and said to him, "You were born totally in sin, and are you trying to teach us?" Then they threw him out.

When Jesus heard that they had thrown him out, he found him and said, "Do you believe in the Son of Man?" He answered and said, "Who is he, sir, that I may believe in him?" Jesus said to him, "You have seen him and the one speaking with you is he." He said, "I do believe, Lord," and he worshiped him. Then Jesus said, "I came into this world for judgment, so that those who do not see might see, and those who do see might become blind."

Some of the Pharisees who were with him heard this and said to him, "Surely we are not also blind, are we?" Jesus said to them, "If you were blind, you would have no sin; but now you are saying, 'We see,' so your sin remains. (Jn 9:1-17, 24-41)

I was showing some guests from a Midwestern state some of the beauty of our part of the country in the Pacific Northwest. In the course of the conversation I asked them what they thought of this portion of God's wonderful world. I was not quite prepared for the answer one of my guests volunteered: "Well, it seems like nice country, but there is one big drawback. You can't see very far, the mountains are in the way."

How true that is also in our spiritual life. We permit certain mountains to obstruct our vision and even blind us to much of the beauty surrounding us. Some of the common obstacles that we face are pride, prejudice, self-centeredness, and insecurity.

When Jesus restored sight to the blind man, the Pharisees refused to believe. They were a proud lot. They refused to acknowledge that Jesus was divine and that he had the power to heal. Yet Jesus stated very clearly: "While I am in the world, I am the light of the world." Since Jesus did not follow all their Pharisaical prescriptions of the law, they rejected him. They accused him of violating their prescriptions of the sabbath. In short, they were blinded to the light.

We can easily be influenced by many of the attitudes which keep us from being receptive to the Lord and what he is asking of us. Our vision may too often be shortsighted. We may be concerned only about our own interests. We may lack a cosmic or eternal view of life. In a way we are blinded to the presence and the power of the Lord in our lives when that happens.

I can sit under a lamp with a three-way light and enjoy reading in its illumination. I also have the option to move farther away from the lamp and to turn my back to the light. Then I will be able to see only obscurely in the dim light. In fact, there is still another avenue open to me. I may walk away from the light altogether into the darkness or close my eyes. Then I will not be able to see at all. I am free to choose any of these options. Just so the Pharisees chose to blind themselves to the miraculous healing power of Jesus. They refused to believe in Jesus.

In this encounter, Jesus also tested the faith of the blind man. When Jesus had smeared the man's eyes with the mud he had mixed with his saliva, he told him: " 'Go wash in the pool of Siloam.'. . . So he went and washed, and came back able to see." Jesus was pleased when the blind man manifested his faith in him. Jesus often reminded the people he had healed that it was their faith which healed them. Their faith opened the way for his saving action in their lives.

There may be blind spots in our own lives of which we are not even aware. We may find it uncomfortable to accept a certain person. Another person may be a threat to us because of our own insecurity. We may be harboring a resentment or prejudice against people of another religious tradition, or race or ethnic origin or political persuasion. Some deep-seated prejudice may be warping our attitudes by its subtle influence. Nothing is more blinding than prejudice which usually arises from ignorance and fear.

In almost all of his confrontations with his enemies, Jesus encountered blind prejudice. They simply refused to accept him and his divine mission because he was a threat to their position. In this episode in the Gospel we can observe prejudice at work again. His enemies could not deny his healing power. It was too evident. They therefore attributed it to the power of the devil.

May we pray daily that our faith be sufficiently strong to remove all the mountains of prejudice which may block out the eternal view of life that God wants to give us. With that eternal view of life in mind, we will be more open to receiving God's healing power in our everyday life.

TWENTY SEVEN

Behold Your Mother

Standing by the cross of Jesus were his mother and his mother's sister, Mary the wife of Clopas, and Mary of Magdala. When Jesus saw his mother and the disciple there whom he loved, he said to his mother, "Woman, behold, your son." Then he said to the disciple, "Behold, your mother." And from that hour the disciple took her into his home. (Jn 19:25-27)

We all need the comfort and care of a mother as children. I am certain that when the boy Jesus hurt himself in the carpenter shop, he ran to his mother for comfort and healing. I am sure that Mary showed him the same loving concern which is typical of mothers the world over.

One of the many reasons why Jesus gave us his mother—as a very precious gift to us from his deathbed on the cross—was so that she might be a comforter and healer for us. How much is contained in that brief statement: "Behold, your mother." Jesus gave us his mother that she might be a healer for us in times of need.

Mary can heal us in many different ways. In the first place, her example and lifestyle is a healing balm for us in the midst of our cluttered and sinful life. Throughout her life she was constantly tested, yet she did whatever God asked of her. She accepted the sword of sorrow prophesied by Simeon. She stood near the cross of Jesus on Calvary as a faithful and loving mother. Her example can be a source of strength and healing for us when afflictions come our way.

Second, Mary obtains healing for us through her powerful intercession before the throne of God, which ministers the healing power of her Son to us. We discover Mary's motherly concern at the wedding feast in Cana. At her special request Jesus changed water into wine to save the embarrassment of the young bride and groom.

Tradition tells us that when Joseph of Arimathea and Nicodemus carefully took down the body of Jesus from the cross, they placed it in the waiting arms of his mother. We commemorate this event in the thirteenth station of the way of the cross. We can envision Mary caressing that lifeless body. She wiped away the blood and grime and lovingly touched every wound and laceration before placing the body of her son in the tomb. The beauty of Michelangelo's Pieta has captured this timeless moment of maternal love for future generations.

That physical body of Jesus symbolizes his spiritual body, the church. Mary is the mother of the church. As a concerned mother, she is aware of all the wounds and lacerations we, the members of the church, are suffering. She fervently intercedes to her son that he would continue to extend his healing power to his kingdom on earth, the church. She also prays with a mother's heart for individual members of the church—each of us—who stand in need of healing. Mary brings comfort and consolation, hope and encouragement, peace and perseverance, to all of her children. As our loving mother she wants us to be healed of the worries, anxieties, and frustrations which beset us.

Mary reminds us at the wedding of Cana of the one thing that is necessary to receive the Lord's healing. We must be cooperative and receptive to the healing power of God. This is what Mary means when she says to each of us as her children: "Do whatever he tells you."

TWENTY EIGHT

Peace Be with You

On the evening of that first day of the week, when the doors were locked, where the disciples were, for fear of the Jews, Jesus came and stood in their midst and said to them, "Peace be with you." When he had said this, he showed them his hands and his side. The disciples rejoiced when they saw the Lord. [Jesus] said to them again, "Peace be with you. As the Father has sent me, so I send you." And when he had said this, he breathed on them and said to them, "Receive the holy Spirit. Whose sins you forgive are forgiven them, and whose sins you retain are retained." (Jn 20:19-23)

An episode of my childhood stands out very vividly in my memory. I had done something that I was forbidden to do. I don't even remember at this date just what it was. My mother was well aware of my misconduct, but she said nothing to me. I waited rather nervously to be corrected by my mother who always did so in a very quiet voice.

Minutes ticked away into hours and no reprimand came. I was feeling more guilty by the moment. I was becoming increasingly more apprehensive. I suppose you could call it my own agony as guilt gnawed away at my conscience.

Finally, I quietly approached my mother who was sitting in her favorite chair mending our clothes with skillful hands. As I approached her chair, she put down her sewing and laid her hand on my shoulder. Looking me straight in the eye she said: "I am so glad God gave you to us and put you in our family." The burden of my guilt suddenly evaporated. My heart soared as she bent down and kissed me.

On the day of the resurrection, Jesus used a similar approach to heal his guilt-ridden disciples. Their hearts were heavy because they had failed him in his final hours with them. They had failed to pray and keep awake with Jesus in the Garden of Gethsemane when he needed their support. When the temple guard and the cohort came to arrest Jesus, they had fled and swiftly disappeared into the late night darkness. With the exception of John they were all conspicuously absent along the way of the cross and at the site of execution on Calvary.

Even though the disciples had locked the doors where they were "for fear of the Jews, Jesus came and stood in their midst." We can well imagine all the thoughts and feelings which welled up within them when they saw the Lord. They must have felt terribly ashamed for having deserted him. Yet mingled with that guilt was their overwhelming joy at seeing him alive. It was too much for them to comprehend.

His very presence was a powerful healing balm for their guilt-laden hearts. They recognized instantly that he had not come to censure them but to reassure them that they were forgiven. His words attest to his mercy and compassion: "Peace be with you." The shalom which Jesus used embraced all the blessings and good things which he wished for them. This included forgiveness and healing.

Jesus went even further. He manifested his loving trust and confidence in them as he gave them an unheard of commission. He not only brought them pardon and peace, but he empowered them to be channels dispensing his forgiveness and healing to others. With the infusion of the Holy Spirit, Jesus conferred upon his first priests the power to forgive sins in his name. Ever since, we have been able to receive forgiveness and healing through the sacrament of penance. The very presence of Jesus must have brought a powerful inner healing to these disciples. An even greater healing took place within them when Jesus manifested his trust and confidence in them by conferring upon them his own divine power to forgive sin.

Jesus is eager and anxious to touch us and heal us in the same way if we come to him with humility and sincerity. Our falls and failings are frequent. We may even wonder if the Lord will forgive us after our frequent protestations of love and our many decisions to avoid certain pitfalls in our life only to fall back into sin. Will he really forgive us again? we may wonder.

Jesus continues to remind us that his love, mercy, and compassion are infinite and that he wants to forgive and heal us more than we want it ourselves. That is the mystery of divine love.

TWENTY NINE

Love Is Patient

Love is patient, love is kind. It is not jealous, [love] is not pompous, it is not inflated, it is not rude, it does not seek its own interests, it is not quick-tempered, it does not brood over injury, it does not rejoice over wrongdoing but rejoices with the truth. It bears all things, believes all things, hopes all things, endures all things. (1 Cor 13:4-7)

Jane and Molly were arriving for their high school senior retreat. As they were entering the building, I overheard Jane say to Molly: "With a face as homely as yours, you will never find a boyfriend." Molly responded to this cutting remark by dashing into the restroom with tears streaming down her face.

Later on during the retreat, Jane asked this question: "If God is so good why is there so much pain and suffering in our lives?" Little did Jane realize that she herself had caused pain and suffering to one of her own classmates just a short time before. Many of our problems are of our own making. Our words are often the chief offender. Either maliciously or unintentionally we can cause another great pain by our speech.

The apostle James does not mince words when he says: "The tongue is also a fire.... With it we bless the Lord and Father, and with it we curse human beings who are made in the likeness of God" (Jas 3:6ff). Our words can devastate another person and even sever a good relationship. On the other hand our words have the power to heal by bringing comfort, peace, and joy to a person in need.

Most of us are concerned about our uncharitableness which stems from our negative or judgmental attitudes. When we recognize our sinfulness in this area and ask the Lord's forgiveness, we can be assured that he will not only forgive us but also begin to heal us from the root cause of these attitudes. At times we may be aware only of our sinfulness in an area which is often a symptom of a deeper problem or sin. If we are to improve we need the Lord's healing in that area which causes us to fail him. Then he can start to work on our root problem, which is likely to go unnoticed otherwise.

By way of example, we may be concerned about our unkindness or our critical remark that brought pain to another person. But we need to look beyond that incident to discover why are we unkind. Our unkindness may arise from various causes. If we are a rather insecure person, our unkindness may be a defense mechanism. Perhaps we may have permitted a resentment to build up within us. Or we may be jealous of another person or envious of someone's good fortune. These are only a few of the many root problems that can cause judgmental and critical attitudes to form in our hearts.

In his classic definition of love, the apostle Paul sets forth a healing process for us. It can serve as an ideal examination of conscience and also help effect a conversion and transformation in our own lives. Let's proceed in this fashion with our own prayer: "Love is patient." Ponder the life of Jesus and recall his infinite patience in dealing with his dull disciples, with hypocritical and merciless enemies and with the eager and energetic little children who were brought to him after an exhausting day. Yes, Jesus was and is very patient.

As our next step in prayer, let's replace the word "love" with a personal pronoun. "Love is patient." Jesus is patient. I should be patient. We may feel a little sting of conscience when we reach this third step, but be assured a healing process is already under way.

As we continue meditating upon this passage with "love is kind," our whole attitude will be transformed. Our mind and heart will be more and more in tune with the heart of Jesus who is the very personification of love. Love, embracing all its component virtues, has a profound healing power.

THIRTY

As the Lord
Has Forgiven You

Put on then, as God's chosen ones, holy and beloved, heartfelt compassion, kindness, humility, gentleness, and patience, bearing with one another and forgiving one another, if one has a grievance against another; as the Lord has forgiven you, so must you also do. And over all these put on love, that is, the bond of perfection. And let the peace of Christ control your hearts, the peace into which you were also called in one body. And be thankful. Let the word of Christ dwell in you richly, as in all wisdom you teach and admonish one another, singing psalms, hymns, and spiritual songs with gratitude in your hearts to God. And whatever you do, in word or in deed, do everything in the name of the Lord Jesus, giving thanks to God the Father through him. (Col 3:12-17)

A heavily drugged man shot and killed Dennis as he was praying in his parish church. He never met Dennis and had no motive for the shooting other than his warped state of mind brought on by the excessive use of drugs. When the police arrived a gun battle ensued in which the young man himself was killed. A few days after the separate funerals of these two victims, Dennis' widow invited the parents of the young man who had killed her husband to accompany her to Mass on Thanksgiving Day. They accepted the invitation even though it was a painful experience for all of them. A great healing took place at that Mass and at the breakfast held afterward. They all found comfort and consolation in this heartfelt sharing of love and forgiveness.

This widow certainly captivated the mind and heart of Christ. She could well have been extremely bitter and unforgiving. She was aware that a true follower of Jesus does not simply follow in the footsteps of the Master but strives to become so much like Jesus that he or she can be identified with him.

Jesus came into our world as a healer. As soon as he began his public ministry, he reached out in healing to everyone in need. In spite of the fact that Jesus spent himself in reaching out to the needy human beings around him, he was not able to accommodate himself to every person who was ill, crippled, or possessed. So he instructed his apostles and then commissioned them to go out to the various villages to heal anyone whom they met. He empowered them when he said: "Cure the sick, raise the dead, cleanse lepers, drive out demons" (Mt 10:8).

Jesus also calls us as his disciples to bring healing to others. The apostle Paul gives us some specific instructions on how we are to carry out this commission. "Put on . . . heartfelt compassion, kindness, humility, gentleness, and patience." In these few words Paul gives us a whole way of life. Jesus' life reflected all these virtues as he went about his divine mission of healing. He healed by his very presence as he radiated compassion, kindness, humility, gentleness, and patience. Jesus urges us to do the same. Anytime Jesus healed physically, he also healed the person spiritually. He always healed the whole person. Joy and praise of God usually rang out after he healed a person.

All of us desperately want forgiveness and healing for ourselves, but we may find it difficult to forgive others. Our unforgiving attitude can hurt another person. If we refuse to recognize another person, or if we shun another person or refuse to speak to him or her or reject someone in any way, we can cause that person much pain. Abraham Lincoln was asked how he intended to treat those who had seceded when the Civil War was over. His response was immediate and truly Christian: "Just like they had never been away."

When we ask another person to forgive us, a great healing takes place within that person and a warm relationship can be restored. In his pastoral admonition the apostle Paul reminds us that our attitude must be the same as Christ's. It will be the same as Jesus' when we are forbearing with one another and forgiving of one another. Paul reminds us that we must forgive others just as the Lord has forgiven us. That is a challenging word.

THIRTY ONE

Equipped for Every Good Work

All scripture is inspired by God and is useful for teaching, for refutation, for correction, and for training in righteousness, so that one who belongs to God may be competent, equipped for every good work. (2 Tm 3:16-17)

I was deeply engrossed in the apostle Paul's Second Epistle to Timothy. His words about the power of the inspired Word of God really impressed me. My meditation was interrupted by the arrival of the mailman. I received a letter from a close friend of mine who is a missionary priest in a far off mission territory. I opened it immediately and read:

"There is a threat of rain in the air right now and a bit of cloudiness to color the afternoon gray. It's the kind of day that seems to have a certain 'Mona Lisa' smile of mystery. And it is the type of ambient I like for writing and for visiting—almost like running to someone to brighten the somberness of the moment, like a child taking hold of Mother's hand in the dark."

He concluded his letter with:

"There comes the threatened rain: thanks for 'taking hold of my hand,' as it were, as I awaited its arrival."

I pondered his words and was reminded of the great healing power words have in our lives. Here we were separated from each other by thousands of miles; yet his writing to me made me very present to him. In turn, as I read his letter he became quite present to me. I could visualize his fingers hitting the keys of his typewriter as he wrote to me. I could almost see his warm and winning smile which has gained him so many friends. It was almost as if I could hear his voice as I read the letter. This is a common experience which all of us have at times when we receive a letter from a close friend or family member.

In such an experience there can be much healing. If we feel a little low at the time, or if we are lonely, such a letter gives us a lift and raises our spirits. It speaks to our heart and gives us the reassurance that we are loved and appreciated.

Did you ever think of the Scriptures not so much as the source of revealed truth, but rather as a personal message from the Lord written to each one of us? In the Vatican Council II, the bishops remind us that Jesus is present in his Word and that it is he himself who is speaking to us when we read his Word (Const Lit #7).

In his Word we find peace and pardon, comfort and consolation, hope and healing. His Word has the power to remove all the worries, anxieties, fears, doubts, and misgivings which many times plague us in daily life. The inspired Word of Scripture is power-packed because Jesus himself is present in his Word. Jesus also affirms the healing power in his Word: "You are already pruned because of the word that I spoke to you" (Jn 15:3).

The words of sacred Scripture also heal by converting our hearts and minds to God. As we expose our thinking and attitudes to the Word of God, we may discover that at times our attitudes, our mind and heart, are not in tune with the mind and heart of Jesus. As we listen prayerfully to his Word, a conversion begins to take place within us, even though we may not be aware of it. This type of conversion is also a healing process effected by his all-powerful Word. This is what the apostle Paul meant when he said that Scripture "is useful for teaching, for refutation, for correction, and for training in righteousness."

In addition to the conversion which takes place within us by the power of God's Word, we ourselves are being transformed so that we may take on more and more the very mindset and heart of Jesus. The Word's transforming and healing power will help us heed Paul's admonition: "Be renewed in the spirit of your minds, and put on the new self, created in God's way in righteousness and holiness of truth" (Eph 4:23-24).

I STEP, I MOUNT: THE VISION OF JOHN HENRY NEWMAN

Edited by Robert Van de Weyer and Pat Saunders

In this selection of extracts, with an extended biographical introduction, we look at the life, ideas and poetry of Cardinal Newman. An Anglican for the first half of his life, Newman became the spiritual leader of the Oxford Movement, seeking sacramental renewal in the Anglican Church. In 1845, he became a Roman Catholic and set out to raise the importance of the laity in the eyes of that church.

THE SPIRITUAL KISS: THE VISION OF SAINT AELRED OF RIEVAULX

Edited by Robert Van de Weyer and Pat Saunders

In this third volume in the Vision of . . . series, the life of Aelred, the official biographer of Edward the Confessor, is considered in the light of his writing. He was a writer in the mystical tradition, severe in his interpretation of the monastic rule but with a genius for friendship. The 'spiritual kiss' to which the title refers is given 'not by the touch of the mouth but by the affection of the heart'.

HIDDEN HEROES OF THE GOSPELS
Feminine Counterparts of Jesus

Joseph A. Grassi

In this fascinating new book, Joseph Grassi studies the Gospels as narrative drama, and discovers that the ideal disciple is often portrayed as a woman. Pursuing a detailed analysis of the literary structure of each of the four Gospels, Grassi shows how the text works to point out the model forms of discipleship, and how women fit this model. Among the women portrayed are the poor widow in the Temple, the daughter of Jairus, the Syro-Phoenician woman, and Mary Magdalene. £4.99

A NON-VIOLENT LIFESTYLE
Conversations with Jean and Hildegard Goss-Mayr

Gérard Houver

Jean and Hildegard Goss-Mayr have spent their lives spreading abroad their message of non-violence. Nominated for the Nobel Peace Prize, they have given seminars throughout the world. £4.99

DRAW NEAR TO GOD
Daily Meditations with Pope John Paul II

In daily meditations throughout the church year, the Pope reflects on the place of marriage, family and work in the Christian's life. He challenges all Christians to respect life, to evangelise and to bring the peace of Christ to a weary world. £4.99

THE WARSAW GHETTO
A Christian's Testimony

Wladyslaw Bartoszewski

Wladyslaw Bartoszewski, a Roman Catholic, offers here a rare testimony to the shared fate of Warsaw's inhabitants during the Holocaust of World War II. His unique and moving book tells the story of the Warsaw ghetto from the unusual perspective of one of the few ethnic Poles to have come to the aid of the Jews during the war. At great peril to his own life, he worked to save some of the Jews and to publicise the events taking place in Poland to an unbelieving world.